Visceral Learning

ALSO BY GERALD JONAS

On Doing Good: The Quaker Experiment

VISCERAL LEARNING

Toward a Science of Self-Control

GERALD JONAS

The Viking Press / New York

To Sarah and Phoebe—the future

Contents

Visceral Learning

The Starting Point

Scientists, despite their passion for objectivity, are as dependent as anyone on subjective judgment when it comes to assessing their colleagues. In the summer of 1969, a fellow scientist referred to Dr. Neal E. Miller of the Rockefeller University in New York as "the best-known experimental psychologist in the country." Although Miller's name was hardly as familiar to the general public as that of the Harvard behavioral psychologist B. F. Skinner, the hyperbole was a tribute to Miller's standing in the professional community and a mark of the importance that scientists attached to his laboratory demonstration of a "new" behavioral phenomenon known as visceral learning. Miller had devoted thirty-five years to the study of how higher animals learn, and he was regarded as a leading theorist for the school of psychology that believes there are general "laws" governing all learning situations—from the hungry white rat searching for food in a maze to the college student cramming for a calculus exam. In his most recent series of experiments, he had shown that white rats could be taught to control many of the bodily functions that had long been regarded by almost everyone—scientists and nonscientists alike—as involuntary. Behind this achievement lay a controversial hypothesis about the nature of the nervous system and more than a decade of research by Miller and a long line of collaborators. In the crucial experiments, rats had learned to work for specific rewards by speeding up or slowing down heartbeat, raising or lowering blood pressure, and increasing or decreasing intestinal contractions. And there was good reason to believe that if rats could learn to modify these functions, so could human beings. This meant that people suffering from hypertension, spastic colon, irregular heartbeats, and other functional disorders might someday be taught to control their own symptoms—from the inside, as it were—without drugs, surgery, or the usual forms of physical therapy. Researchers who shared Miller's basic outlook were already investigating some of these practical applications. But the first experiments that Miller and his co-workers ran with human subjects only pointed up how much basic research remained to be done, and how little anyone really knew about the fundamental relationship of the brain, the body, and the outside world.

What originally intrigued me about Miller's work on visceral learning was not the results of those experiments but the fact that they were being done at all. Here was an eminent experimental psychologist delving into a phenomenon—the voluntary control of internal bodily functions—that I had always associated with the meditative exercises of yoga and Zen Buddhism. I am neither a scientist nor a mystic, but it was my impression that nothing could be more alien to the spirit of Eastern mysticism than the methods of Western experimental science—especially behavioral science. According to the popular stereotype, the behaviorist views the living organism as a complicated machine; by working out the precise relationship between "input" and "output," he hopes to achieve the ability to predict and control human behavior. The mystic, according to another stereotype, contemplates his own navel in an effort to become "one" with the Infinite. (The word *yoga* in Sanskrit means "union" or "yoke.") These two approaches to the mysteries of human existence appear to be totally incompatible. Yet appearances, as both scientists and mystics like to remind us, can be deceiving.

One of the myths of Western civilization is that pure science—as opposed to applied science, or technology—is essentially neutral in its influence on men's lives. In this view, pure science merely gives us the power to act out our desires on a grand scale; what we choose to do with this power is a question of *values*, which are beyond the province of scientific thought. In one sense, of course, this is a truism: Atomic energy can kill or cure, annihilate cities or make the desert bloom. But there is another, deeper sense in which pure science is constantly involved with value judgments, and to ignore this dimension of the scientific enterprise is to miss the whole point of the extraordinary new discoveries being made in experimental psychology today.

Men could not even disagree among themselves about moral and social issues unless they shared certain basic assumptions about the nature of reality; and in our culture we look to science to draw the line between what is a fact and what is not. Our private experiences—no matter how vivid—have no public validity unless science takes official notice of them in one way or another. And since there is never enough time (and there are never enough resources) to investigate everything, the first step in the validation process is to decide whether or not a particular experience —or class of experiences—is worth looking into. This crucial decision is not necessarily made on purely scientific grounds. Indeed, entire areas of human experience may be excluded from the scrutiny of science because of what Neal

Miller calls the "cultural prejudice" of the scientists themselves. For example: Practitioners of yoga and Zen meditation have always had the reputation of being able to alter their internal bodily processes at will. Until recently Western scientists refused to take such reports seriously, partly because they had no instruments to evaluate the evidence objectively, and partly because the claims of the yogis and Zen masters made sense only in a cultural context very different from that in which Western science had flourished. While the voluntary control of internal organs is hardly the goal of Eastern mysticism, it is characteristic of the Eastern emphasis on achieving self-fulfillment through self-discipline.* By contrast, the whole thrust of the scientific enterprise in the West has been to achieve mastery over the external conditions of life. To make this task easier, we have learned to think of our bodies, and even of our minds, as objects in a world governed by mathematically exact laws. We assume that such laws exist, even if our present attempts to express them are only rough approximations. There is no denying that this intellectual strategy has been extraordinarily useful in many ways. But social critics like Lewis Mumford point out that our very success in predicting and controlling the behavior of objects has led to a dangerous imbalance. One obvious symptom of this imbalance is the disdain with which our most famous behavioral scientists, from John B. Watson to B. F. Skinner, have treated the "facts" of man's subjectivity.

Civilized men have always struggled to reconcile objective knowledge with subjective experience—if only because they assume that a course of action based exclusively on one or the other is not likely to succeed. But the more

---

*"We discern in the yoga those cardinal conceptions of Hindu thought, such as the supremacy of the psychic over the physical, the exaltation of silence and solitude, meditation and ecstasy, and the indifference to outer conditions, which make the traditional Hindu attitude toward life appear so strange and fantastic to the modern mind"—Sarvepalli Radhakrishnan, in *Indian Philosophy* (1927).

successful the scientific enterprise in the West became, the easier it was to downgrade the value of subjective experience. What a man felt was believed to be of little importance compared to what he did; science provided the tools, and it was taken for granted that mental states such as consciousness and volition were inaccessible to scientific probing. (The psychoanalytical theories of Freud were acceptable only in the clinic—and in literary criticism—while the phenomenon of hypnosis was relegated to the status of a parlor trick.)

As long as the immediate benefits of the Western scientific enterprise clearly outweighed any potential dangers, there was no compelling reason to quarrel with its underlying value judgments. The great majority of mankind has always been ill-fed, ill-housed and disease-ridden; science held out the promise of alleviating these conditions. During most of the nineteenth century and the first half of the twentieth, it was possible to believe that problems arising from the abuse of technology were essentially self-correcting: whenever one machine gave us trouble, science could be relied on to build a better, safer, more efficient replacement. Both Marxists and capitalists could agree that the horrors of the Industrial Revolution were a temporary aberration, a stage of development to be outgrown with the aid of science. By calling their socialism "scientific" as opposed to Utopian, the Marxists stressed that they were interested in results, not pipe-dreams. Everyone knew that science *worked.* Its progress was exponential; there were no theoretical limits to its power. Of course there were other voices—writers, philosophers, clerics—who warned against an uncritical "scientism." But since such warnings were often interwoven with nostalgia for a romanticized past, they could be easily dismissed as elitist and unrealistic. The *real* flaw in scientism became clear only after the Second World War, when we discovered that science had given us

enough power to destroy the world, and the scientists discovered that their creations (like Dr. Frankenstein's) were
out of control.

Like most people I know, I cannot help feeling ambiva-
lent about the announcement of a new "scientific breakthrough." My vision of the scientist keeps shifting from
Omniscient Sorcerer to Technician of Death and back
again. I am grateful for my full refrigerator and my antibiot-
ics and my labor-saving devices, and I would genuinely like
to find out if there is life on Mars. But I cringe at the clouds
of pollutants pouring from factories and power plants, and
I go out of my way to buy foods that have received the
minimum of processing, and I try to think as little as possible about the automated nuclear arsenals and the fail-safe
mechanisms that guard them. I cannot imagine living without the benefits of science, but I am aware that it is getting
harder and harder to live with them. In the past year two
different teams of concerned scientists—one in England
and one in the United States—have tried to project recent
trends in population, production, and consumption into
the future, using the most up-to-date techniques of computer simulation. The conclusions drawn from the two
studies are remarkably consistent: The highly industrial-
ized countries of the West cannot continue on their present
course without precipitating a worldwide disaster: Even if
we somehow manage to avert a nuclear showdown (and
with the increasing competition for the earth's limited resources, the odds are not exactly encouraging) we have
only a few decades left in which to save our planet's life-
support systems from irreparable damage.

Not every concerned scientist accepts these "doomsday"
predictions in all their details. The influential British journal *Nature* described the Malthusian models used in both
studies as "over-simple" and "confusing." But it is clear

that we are in the midst of a crisis of confidence in the Western world. By our own admission, we have become dangerous to ourselves and to the rest of mankind. We have the word of experts that technological expertise alone cannot bring our runaway technology under control. As Barry Commoner says in *The Closing Circle,* "everything is connected to everything else." Merely building a safer car, or passing a few anti-pollution bills, or limiting the number of ICBMs in underground silos will not save us. According to the sponsors of one of the doomsday studies, "any deliberate attempt to reach a rational and enduring state of equilibrium by planned measures rather than by chance or catastrophe must ultimately be founded on a basic change of values and goals at individual, national and world levels."*

From now on, it seems, we must scale down our expectations. We must learn to be satisfied with a smaller pie, and to share even that with our less fortunate neighbors. In short, if we want to survive, we must begin to develop habits of self-control that have been all but forgotten in the West during the great technological binge of the last century and a half.

Among other things, this new cultural imperative should force us to reappraise the introspective "prescientific" view of man that has been associated with the mystical religions of India, China, and Japan for thousands of years. Eastern mysticism not only assumes that a man must be fully self-aware to live in harmony with his surroundings; it also provides specific techniques for achieving and maintaining this awareness. While the techniques vary greatly from sect to sect and from teacher to teacher (and the ultimate goal may be described in strikingly diverse metaphors), there is one common element: The novice is expected to transcend

* *The Limits to Growth,* Potomac Associates (1972).

his false image of himself as a conscious-but-intangible
mind somehow tacked onto a tangible-but-insensible body.
Once free of this dualistic delusion, a man may come to see
himself as a fully integrated being in continuous give-and-
take with the rest of the cosmos, as an integral part of some
vast cosmic entity. A handful of Western converts have
found it possible to follow the traditional Eastern paths
toward this "enlightenment."* But it is unlikely that yoga
and Zen in their traditional forms—lotus positions, koans,
mantras, mendicant holy men, and so on—will ever have a
significant impact on Western civilization. The barriers of
history and language are too formidable. And even if we
could get past these, we can hardly afford to abandon our
heritage just now, when we need so many of our technological skills to *undo* the damage we have already done. Nor
would it make much sense to become imitation Eastern
mystics at the very moment when the East is adapting Western science, along with Western ideologies, to its own
needs. Fortunately, cultural cross-fertilization does not imply a simple-minded mimicry. The flaws in both traditions
are only too evident: If Western science gained the whole
world only to lose its soul, Eastern mysticism turned inward
to seek enlightenment while its children starved. In redefin-
ing our goals, we are free to weave the strengths of both
traditions into a civilization capable of overcoming famine,
disease, and other natural disasters while maintaining the
self-discipline that prevents the abuse of such powers. But
we will have to find the materials for this synthesis in our
own intellectual heritage. There is no way to predict what
kind of society will emerge from the incredible ferment in
India, China, and Japan, except that these countries will
certainly not be carbon copies of England, Russia, or the
United States. The Japanese may find a way to tame indus-

*"To see directly into one's original Nature, that is Zen"—quoted from a
classic Chinese text by D. T. Suzuki in *Zen Buddhism* (1956).

trial growth before they choke on their industrial waste, or they may not. The Chinese may reconcile economic development with an ethos that puts state ahead of self, or they may not. In any case, we cannot wait to find out, because it is the technology of the West that poses the most immediate threat to mankind. Innumerable prophets have told us we must change, or die. The only question is how. The thesis of this book is that our best hope of making ourselves over in the short time available is not to renounce science and all its works but to concentrate on becoming better scientists.

At a certain stage in the development of any science, specialization is a tactical necessity. For example, in their attempt to unravel the complexities of human behavior, the early experimental psychologists concentrated on a few easily observed, and therefore easily controlled, variables. But B. F. Skinner notwithstanding, the era of a narrowly conceived behaviorism appears to be coming to an end. A parallel can be drawn to recent developments in physics, chemistry, and biology. As knowledge proliferates, the neat divisions between disciplines are increasingly seen as obstacles to further progress, until there is no choice but to widen the focus—even if this means sacrificing the apparent clarity of earlier work. Fortified with insights gained through a systematic investigation of relatively simple behavior, psychologists like Neal Miller have begun to map out a much more ambitious program, one that looks forward to a genuinely objective study of *all* aspects of human experience, including those experiences that have usually been labeled subjective.

Two prominent experimental psychologists—Joe Kamiya of the Langley Porter Neuropsychiatric Institute in San Francisco, and Johann Stoyva of the University of Colorado Medical Center—have suggested that a prototype for the scientific study of subjective phenomena may be found in the field of dream research. Presumably, everyone dreams. But not everyone remembers his dream accurately or tells the truth about what he remembers. These difficulties do not discourage the psychoanalyst, who is as interested in the distortions of the telling as he is in the dream material itself. Until a few years ago, however, most experimental psychologists shied away from a field in which the only data available were the unsupported verbal reports of subjects trying to describe what had been going on in their minds while they were asleep. Then, in 1952, two physiologists discovered a curious correlation between reported dream memories and the cyclic bursts of rapid eye movements (REMs) that occur during certain stages of sleep. When a person is awakened during or immediately after an REM episode, he almost invariably reports that he has been dreaming. Furthermore, his rapid eye movements —which can be reliably monitored by laboratory instruments—often parallel the reported action of the dream. For instance, after a burst of horizontal eye movements, the subject may report that he dreamed of watching a tennis match; after a burst of vertical eye movements, he may report that he dreamed of watching a bouncing ball. Since a dreamer is never aware of his rapid eye movements as such, he presumably cannot fake their appearance; because of this, the REM bursts soon came to be accepted as an objective indicator of the subjective state of dreaming. Discovery of this "REM indicator" suddenly made dream research "respectable" to experimental psychologists. It was not necessary to prove that dreams cause REMs or that REMs cause dreams. It was not even necessary to prove that REMs always accompany dreams. (In fact, there is reason to believe that dreams can sometimes occur without REMs and vice versa.) What brought about the change in attitude was simply the close convergence of REM episodes and dream reports. Stoyva and Kamiya see this as an example of the "logic of converging operations," a bold research strategy that has produced excellent results in the physical sciences. When experimental evidence from a variety of sources points to a serious gap in our understanding of the basic properties of matter and energy, physicists and biologists do not hesitate to fill the gap with a specially designed "hypothetical construct." Both the atom and the gene have been employed as hypothetical constructs. "The important point," according to Stoyva and Kamiya, "is that neither of these concepts is fully indexed by any one [experimental] operation, but is an inference built up on the basis of many intersecting and overlapping observations. Similarly we may conceive of dreaming as a hypothetical construct . . . which is indexed in a less than perfect way by *both* verbal reports and REMs." In psychology, any frequently reported subjective experience can be treated as a hypothetical construct. And the closer the correlation between what a person says is going on in his mind and what the instruments reveal is going on in his body, the more secure one feels in attributing objective validity to that person's "mental state."

This analysis may seem tedious to the layman who does not need to be convinced that dreams exist. But what about the radical changes in consciousness that are reported to take place during the practice of yoga and Zen meditation? The ultimate expression of Western skepticism on such matters comes from Freud himself: "There is no appeal beyond reason. And if the truth of religious doctrines is dependent on an inner experience which bears witness to that truth, what is one to make of the many people who do not have that rare experience? . . . Of what significance is it for other people that you have won from a state of ecstasy . . . an imperturbable conviction of the real truth of the doctrines of religion?" Of course, most Eastern religions

stress that a certain period of mental and physical prepara-
tion is necessary before the seeker can experience the
"truth." But the Western skeptic will hardly concede this
point on the basis of hearsay alone. Freud, who dealt so
comfortably with such hypothetical constructs as dreams
and neuroses, saw no reason to accept the testimony of the
mystics, because he had never had any mystical experiences
of his own and because he knew of no methods for objectively identifying someone else's mystical experience.

Such methods now exist. Scientists who have studied the
electroencephalographic (EEG) records of yogis and Zen
monks during meditation have detected "brain-wave" patterns not normally found in waking, drowsy, or sleeping
subjects, or in people under hypnotic trance. Further support for the claim that *something* happens to the organism
during a mystical experience comes from research in the
new field of biofeedback training. In the late 1950s, for
example, Joe Kamiya proved that when people were informed about the electrical activity of the brain through an
EEG feedback system, they could learn to control a specific
brain-wave pattern—the alpha rhythm—and that such control was often associated with subjective experiences of the
type described in the literature of Eastern mystical religions. Other studies have shown that "consistent and pro-
nounced physiologic changes" occur during the practice of
a simplified yoga-like technique called transcendental
meditation.

The impact of such research on traditional Western attitudes toward both science and mysticism has yet to be
gauged. From all accounts, the 1960s saw an increased
interest in Eastern meditative disciplines among young
people—but there have been similar waves of enthusiasm
in the past. Electronic feedback devices for do-it-yourself
alpha training in the home are selling briskly—but so were

water beds last year (or was it the year before?). There is no way to tell whether these trends signify anything more profound than the search for new ways of getting high; unfortunately, a path that leads to enlightenment in one culture may lead all too easily to escapism in another.

A Zen master once said, "Before a man studies Zen, to him mountains are mountains and waters are waters; after he gets an insight into the truth of Zen through the instruction of a good master, mountains to him are *not* mountains and waters are *not* waters; but after this, when he really attains to the abode of rest, mountains are once more mountains and waters are waters." The curious paradoxes of Zen literature are a deliberate attempt to undermine a man's faith in his abstract reasoning ability and to prepare him for an encounter with "subjectively" perceived truth. But it must be remembered that this method of instruction was designed with a specific audience in mind. Suzuki and other commentators emphasize that the mystical literature of Mahayana Buddhism was completely reinterpreted by the Chinese Zen masters, and that Japanese Zen has undergone a further transformation. It is not surprising that most Westerners find this literature impenetrable. When asked to explain the essence of Zen, another ancient master said, "Your ordinary, everyday mind, that is Zen." But the ordinary, everyday mind of the West is saturated with science, all the way down to the level where we decide what is "reality" and what is "illusion." I cannot hear the paradox about the mountains and the waters without interpreting it in the light of what I know about modern physics: Matter and energy are interchangeable; mountains and rivers are whirls of infinitesimal particles held together in space by certain forces of interaction; to get a glimpse of these forces interacting is to get a glimpse of what matter and energy really are. Whether or not this interpretation violates the spirit of Zen is beside the point. Our appreciation of the

insights of other cultures will come through the medium of
science or not at all. On similar grounds, Carl Jung warned
against the "application of yoga to the peoples of the West.
. . . Western civilization is scarcely a thousand years old and
must first of all free itself from its barbarous one-sidedness.
This means, above all, deeper insight into the nature of
man. But no insight is gained . . . by imitating methods
which have grown up under totally different psychological
conditions."

Before we can change ourselves, we must know who we
are. The importance of biofeedback research is that it ad-
dresses itself rigorously to both these goals, in language
that the layman can understand if he makes the effort. The
basic principle of biofeedback training is perfectly compati-
ble with the Western emphasis on achieving mastery over
the external conditions of life: If you know the results of
your past performance, you can improve your future performance. Parents and teachers apply this principle to their
everyday tasks without thinking about it. The same principle is also basic to modern communications theory, computer technology, and systems engineering. To take a very
simple example, an "automatic pilot" changes the position
of a ship's rudders whenever feedback signals show that the
actual course of the ship is deviating from a desired course
that has been programed into the device.

In a paradox worthy of the ancient Zen masters, biofeedback researchers have discovered that living organisms can
modify many supposedly involuntary bodily functions if
they are guided by external signals that tell them what is
happening inside their bodies from moment to moment.
When it comes to interpreting this discovery, scientists
tend to divide into two camps: one group, drawing on
communications theory, stresses the purely informational
aspect of the feedback signals; the other group, drawing on
behaviorist learning theory, stresses the role of the feed-

back signals in reinforcing appropriate responses. No matter what their theoretical position, however, most biofeedback researchers cite the visceral-learning experiments of Neal Miller as a milestone in the field, and Miller's research was conceived and carried out entirely within a behaviorist framework. The story behind this intellectual adventure is worth telling in detail, because it shows how Western science can take a long, hard look at some cherished assumptions of Western civilization, without cutting itself adrift from the traditional strengths of Western thought.

1

The Wiggling of One Ear

Most people think of learning as a conscious mental process, a deliberate attempt to grasp an abstract principle ("The square of the hypotenuse is equal to the sum of the squares of the other two sides") or to master a special skill involving the so-called skeletal muscles of the limbs, the torso, and the head (driving a car, hitting a golf ball, singing on key). At first glance, visceral learning appears to be something else entirely. For example, the circulation of blood through the arteries and veins, even in a severe case of hypertension, produces no consciously perceived sensations. This means that before a person can even begin to learn to control his blood pressure he has to be provided with some kind of artificial feedback, through a monitoring device akin to the inflatable rubber cuff that physicians use to gauge blood pressure. The monitoring device can be rigged to let the patient know whenever his blood pressure drops significantly, but there is no way to make him *feel* what is happening inside his body. Learning to control the body's cardiovascular machinery under these conditions would be a little like learning to make love by correspondence course.

Despite these obvious difficulties, some of the subjects in Neal Miller's early experiments at Rockefeller University did learn to reduce their blood pressure on cue, though they were unable to explain what they had done or how they had done it. The subjects themselves compared their newly acquired skill to feats of bodily control reportedly performed by Indian yogis or by people in deep hypnotic trances. Miller found these parallels fascinating and definitely worth further investigation. But this did not mean he shared the view of his subjects that visceral learning was some kind of behavioral anomaly; in fact, his analysis of the phenomenon had already led him to the opposite conclusion; that the most interesting thing about visceral learning was its similarity to ordinary learning.

In objective terms, the lowest common denominator of all learning is a change in behavior resulting from an encounter with the outside world. In the case of the skeletal muscles, this process begins in early infancy; we observe infants making repeated passes at an offered rattle or shying away from an object that has been associated with an unpleasantly loud noise or bright light. But since we retain no memory of our own "basic training" in the use of the skeletal muscles, we tend to think of the learning process in terms of later, more sophisticated manifestations. For instance, we say that we are "starting from scratch" when we take up some new activity like driving a car or playing golf. No matter how helpless we may look and feel during our first lesson, however, we already have at our fingertips most of the tools we need. Years of experience in grappling with our environment have taught us that a little more tension in *these* fingers will give us a little better control *here*, and bending the wrist in *that* direction will provide a little more flexibility *there*. By contrast, our glands and internal organs are normally so well insulated from learning encounters that the average person goes through life with hardly any more control over his visceral functions than a newborn baby. If Miller was right, the human volunteers in his visceral-learning experiments were being thrust into a kind of second childhood, where they were discovering on their own what a few experimental psychologists had always contended in theory—that consciousness was "an unnecessary hypothesis" when one got down to the bare bones of the learning process. In other words, there was nothing strange about acquiring muscular skills without conscious control; it was simply learning on the most basic level.

Even Miller, however, had difficulty imagining what learning on this level might be like. One way to satisfy his curiosity would have been to use himself as a subject for a visceral-learning experiment. But he appeared to be a particularly unsuitable subject, since his heart rate and blood pressure were unusually steady. Besides, as the head of a major laboratory in which fifteen Ph.D.s and twelve technicians were working on a number of other important projects in addition to visceral learning—all supported by grants from the National Institute of Mental Health—Miller had only a limited amount of time to spare. So he looked around for some informal experiment that he could perform on himself outside the laboratory—something involving a simple skeletal response that was almost as far removed from the mainstream of human learning experiences as blood-pressure control. While his experimental subjects were working to control their glands and internal organs, Dr. Miller set out to teach himself to wiggle one of his ears without moving the other.

• • • •

On Friday, March 20, 1970, a thirty-two-year-old woman suffering from an excruciating headache was taken to the emergency room of New York Hospital–Cornell Medical Center by ambulance. The young woman, Robin Bielski, had awakened the previous Saturday with a dull ache in the back of her head and neck. She had had a few drinks with friends the night before, but it seemed to her that the ache was in the wrong place for a hangover. In any event, she went to her regular Saturday-morning gym class, where, under supervision, she practiced forward somersaults, headstands, and other exercises designed to develop graceful posture and to help city-dwellers "learn to know their bodies better." Afterward, Miss Bielski noticed increased pain and stiffness in her neck. Over the next few days, the pain got progressively worse. She went to her regular doctor, and he referred her to a neurologist. The neurologist performed a spinal tap—a standard diagnostic test for damage to the central nervous system. The results were negative. The usual medications for a severe headache were prescribed—codeine, Darvon, Demerol—but nothing gave her relief. On Tuesday, Miss Bielski, who was a copywriter for an advertising agency, was unable to go to work. She could not eat, and she had trouble sleeping. Any head movement made the pain worse. By Thursday, she had begun to feel dizzy all the time. No longer able to take care of herself (she lived alone in a fifth-floor walkup), she telephoned her mother, who lives in Philadelphia. Her mother arrived Thursday night. On Friday morning, Mrs. Bielski put in a call to the neurologist and explained the situation. The doctor told her to get her daughter to the hospital right away.

• • • •

Compared with other skeletal responses that have a high survival value—like running and reaching and grasping—the average person's control of his ear-wiggling apparatus is almost completely undeveloped. Many people are unable to wiggle their ears at all. Some, like Miller, are amused to discover during their childhood that they can wiggle both ears in unison. But wiggling one ear without moving the other is a surprisingly difficult feat of coordination that can be appreciated only by someone who has tried to master it. As an experimental psychologist known for his contributions to modern learning theory, Miller at least had a pretty good idea of what to expect. The problem, as he defined it for himself, was "to bring the wiggling response of the right ear under more specific stimulus control." While this formulation did not guarantee success, it was helpful in explaining to Mrs. Miller why her eminent husband could be found from time to time staring intently at his reflection in a bathroom mirror.

Miller could "tell" both his ears to wiggle in unison, and he knew that the muscles were responding correctly, because he could see the movement in the mirror and could also feel it. The fact that some people could wiggle their ears independently showed that it was physiologically possible to break this response down into a right and a left component, but Miller also knew that no one—not even an ear-wiggling virtuoso—could guide him toward this goal, for the simple reason that there are no commonly accepted cue words for the necessary muscular adjustments. Parents who have tried to teach a two-year-old child to blow his nose or to drink through a straw will recognize the problem; the child is born with the ability to blow air out through his nose and to suck air in through his mouth, but he has not yet learned to associate these actions with specific instructions. The would-be ear-wiggler may know the Latin name for every muscle and nerve in the head, but this will not help him if he has never learned to attach a physical response to the words.

For his personal training program in ear-control, Miller

adopted a method of step-by-step instruction that he had
used successfully with rats, dogs, and human beings in the
visceral-learning experiments. This method—which is
known as instrumental, or operant, conditioning—is based
on the familiar observation that immediate rewards influence future behavior. Animal trainers, for example, know
that a hungry dog will work for food. To teach a dog to sit
up on the command "Beg!" the trainer tosses the animal
a piece of food every time it makes the correct response. If
the trainer is patient enough, the dog will eventually learn
to do whatever is instrumental—from *its* point of view—in
getting the reward. The dog will also learn to avoid certain
actions if it is punished whenever it makes an incorrect
response—the reward in this case being the cessation of
punishment as soon as the incorrect response ceases. Experimental psychologists prefer to describe this whole
training process in terms that do not require unverifiable
hypotheses about what is going on inside the dog's head.
They speak of a reward as "reinforcing" the connection
between a response (sitting up) and a stimulus (the command "Beg!"). A "reinforced response" is simply one that
is more likely to recur the next time the stimulus is repeated. Exactly how the reinforcing effect is achieved inside
the learning organism is one of the great mysteries of the
life sciences, but it is not hard to see what role the mechanism of reinforcement plays in the individual's daily life.
There is a close parallel to the process of natural selection
in the life of the species. In general, higher organisms tend
to repeat those patterns of behavior which are instrumental
in satisfying physical needs, avoiding pain, and relieving
stress and tension in the nervous system. A white rat trying
to escape an electric shock, a hungry dog sitting up on
command, a baby reaching for a teething ring, a psychologist trying to prove a point by wiggling his ear—in all these
cases the underlying mechanism of reinforcement is as-

sumed to be the same. In laymen's terms, all four learners are working, whether they know it or not, for rewards.

Laymen and many scientists refer to the initial stages of the process as "trial-and-error" learning, but from the point of view of modern learning theory this is something of a misnomer. Each error leads only to the elimination of a fruitless response and therefore to another trial; to get learning, you need successful trials, suitably reinforced. In fact, the most difficult part of the trainer's job can be waiting for the subject to perform the first correct response—or, if the response is quite an elaborate one, even some small part of it—so that a reward can be administered. This was what kept Miller in front of the bathroom mirror. According to his own understanding of the laws of learning, his chances of teaching himself to wiggle one ear were almost nil unless he could catch himself in the act—even the faintest flutter of independent movement would do—and immediately reinforce this spontaneous wiggle with a burst of self-congratulation.

• • • •

The first physician to examine Miss Bielski in the emergency room of New York Hospital jotted down the words "Probably migraine" on her admission papers. He also noted the possibility of aseptic meningitis or of a subarachnoid hemorrhage (bleeding inside the cranial cavity). Miss Bielski was placed under observation in the neurology department and given what hospitals call a complete workup. The results of the first series of tests and examinations seemed to point to some kind of spinal injury in the neck region, possibly as a result of overstrenuous exercise. The patient had a history of hypertension, however, so there was also some concern about her blood pressure, which was slightly higher than normal. Then, during the next twenty-four hours, more specific, and more serious, symptoms appeared. Little by little, Miss Bielski lost control of the left side of her body. Another spinal tap was taken; this time traces of blood were found in the cerebrospinal fluid. An arteriogram revealed a dark mass in the left hemisphere of the cerebellum, a brain structure, situated toward the back of the skull, that is concerned with the coordination of skeletal muscles and with the maintenance of posture and muscle tone. Now it became apparent that Miss Bielski had suffered a cerebellar hemorrhage. An operation to relieve the internal pressure caused by the blood-engorged brain tissue was ordered immediately. While she was being prepared for surgery, the patient lost consciousness for the first time. In the course of the operation, the neurosurgeon removed a small piece of the skull to expose the cerebellum, and then cut out the hemorrhagic swelling, which was not only interfering with cerebellar functions but also pressing down on the "alertness center" in the brain stem. After the operation, Miss Bielski remained in a coma. There was no way of knowing how much damage had been done or what her condition would be when she returned to consciousness.

•   •   •   •

The image that stared back at Miller from the mirror was of a stocky, outdoorsy man, bald except for a white fringe behind the ears, with ruddy cheeks, a firm jaw, a broad nose, and deep-set green eyes, which did not need corrective lenses. Born in 1909, he was a member of what might be called the third generation of American behavioral scientists; he had been associated with Yale University for more than thirty years before moving to the Rockefeller University in 1966. Much of his career had been spent teaching white rats and other laboratory animals to make simple physical responses (pressing a bar, spinning a wheel) in order to earn concrete rewards (a pellet of food, a sip of water). Underlying this work was a modern theory of learning that began with an almost total rejection of the "introspective" approach of classical psychology.

The experimental psychologists of the early twentieth century, in aspiring to the methodological purity of physics and chemistry, turned their backs on all forms of inquiry that did not allow verification by other investigators. Since there was obviously no way to verify someone's account of his own thoughts and feelings, the systematic study of human consciousness—a touchstone of nineteenth-century psychology—was dropped from the syllabus. What replaced it was the systematic study of overt behavior. Thoughts and feelings were recognized as important only insofar as they found expression in observable activity. Still, implicit in this new approach, which came to be known as behaviorism, was a challenge to take over the subject matter of the old, introspective psychology by restating it in a set of purely "operational" definitions. Unlike a dictionary definition, an operational definition of a phenomenon does not necessarily describe or explain. Rather, it provides a lever for *manipulating* the phenomenon in a specified setting. For example, everyone knows what the sensation of fear is, and Webster's New International Dictionary (Second Edition) gives an adequate descriptive definition: "Painful emotion marked by alarm, extreme awe, or anticipation of danger." But a researcher interested in fear as a determinant of behavior needs something more concrete; he wants something he can observe directly and measure objectively. From this standpoint, the most useful information about psychological variables like fear has come from a stimulus-response analysis of behavior. A researcher working with white rats might make the following observation: When a rat is turned loose in a cage where it was previously given a strong electric shock through a metal grid in the floor, the rat scrambles about, trying to escape, even though the current in the grid has been turned off. Since the rat is not now receiving shock, it appears to be motivated by the fear of a second shock; presumably, the more frightened the rat, the harder it will try to escape. These statements sound reasonable; indeed, they verge on truism. What is important about them is that, taken together, they point to a prediction about future behavior that can be stated in strictly objective terms: the stronger the original shock, the more vigorous the animal's escape responses will become. This statement requires no subjective judgments; it can be proved or disproved by the use of a simple restraining harness that allows the investigator to measure the animal's pulling strength after it has received shocks of varying voltage. Of course there is bound to be a lower limit below which the shock is too weak to produce any observable effect on the rat's behavior, and there will also be an upper limit above which the shock is so strong that the animal simply freezes. But if the predicted correlation between shock strength and pulling strength does hold true over a clearly defined middle range, the researcher can assume that he is getting an objective fix on the subjective experience commonly called fear.

Once a particular operational definition is shown to be reliable within given limits, it can be used as a yardstick to measure other aspects of behavior. For example, the researcher may adapt the pulling-strength criterion to test the hypothesis that certain drugs, like alcohol, substantially weaken the fear response (as the colloquial phrase "Dutch courage" suggests). Or the researcher may use the criterion to determine whether an electric shock that is preceded by a warning buzzer produces stronger fear than a shock that comes without any warning. Eventually, from a small but carefully cross-checked body of data on the behavior of the frightened white rat, the researcher can advance to predictions about the behavior of the frightened human being.

Rigorous pursuit of this strategy has helped to liberate researchers from culture-bound dogmas and unexamined assumptions about behavior that had long masqueraded as "common sense." But scientists are only human, and the history of behavioral psychology in the United States offers a cautionary lesson in the pitfalls of objectivity. Encouraged by their initial success in manipulating a few simple laboratory situations, some early behaviorists rushed to elevate a perfectly sound research strategy into a new intellectual dogma. All subjective phenomena that could not be operationally defined with the techniques then available were set aside. Before long, the failure of behaviorism to deal with such phenomena was taken as a sign not that the available techniques were inadequate but that the phenomena themselves were irrelevant, and in this way many of the mental processes that the scientists themselves prized most highly, including self-awareness, abstract reasoning, imagination, and creativity, were virtually excluded from serious consideration.

Among his colleagues Miller has a reputation for carrying out painstaking behavioral research in areas of major importance and for reporting his findings with precision and circumspection. Yet his attitude toward the shibboleths of modern behaviorism has been anything but doctrinaire. Unlike many of his predecessors and contemporaries, he can be refreshingly candid about the interplay of fact and theory in scientific research. "Pure empiricism is a delusion," he has written. "Gathering all the facts with no bias from theory is utterly impossible. Scientists are forced to make a drastic selection, either unconsciously on the basis of perceptual habits and the folklore and linguistic categories of the culture, or consciously on the basis of explicitly formulated theory." And in his technical articles, as if to remind himself (and the reader) of the tentative nature of all scientific theory, he goes out of his way to detail the particular assumptions on which he has proceeded and to present a brief critique of the strengths and weaknesses of his theoretical position. He will even offer odds on the likelihood that one of his assumptions will turn out to be incorrect: "Although I believe that the foregoing hypothesis has a considerably less than 50-per-cent chance of being correct," he wrote in one paper, "I do believe it is better at the present moment than any other single hypothesis." When he runs into unexpected trouble—as he has recently in replicating some of the early animal experiments in visceral learning—his reports to the scientific community are every bit as candid and precise as those dealing with his most successful work.

In the long run, Miller believes, the task of behavioral psychology is to lay the groundwork for a much broader science—"a unified science of human behavior," which will draw on the techniques and insights of physiology, zoology, biochemistry, anthropology, psychiatry, and cybernetics, among other disciplines—and he feels that the young scientists now emerging from the colleges and graduate schools take naturally to such a multidisciplinary approach. In 1966, to encourage this trend, Miller set up a laboratory of physiological psychology at Rockefeller. Typical of the young people working with him today is a twenty-nine-year-old researcher in the life sciences named Barry Dworkin, who brings to the visceral-learning project an impressive schooling in physiology, a thorough grounding in Freudian theory, and a knack for designing and building the complex electronic hardware that has become indispensable to the modern behavioral laboratory.

Miller readily admits that he does not consciously apply

the insights of learning theory in his relationship with his graduate students. As he puts it, the job of teaching graduate students falls "halfway between the realm of art and the realm of science," since creative scientific research involves "complex motivations and responses that we know very little about." He adds, "You can try to sharpen the problems for your students and help them avoid blind alleys, but essentially you have to give them practice in learning things on their own. Unfortunately, there is a type of teacher who tends to put a ceiling on the development of his students by implying that they can never hope to learn as much as he has. It so happens that out of necessity—because I have such a wide range of interests and keep getting involved in new areas—I regularly expect my students to know more than I do about at least one field. And I expect them to be able to put this knowledge to work in the laboratory." One of his greatest rewards in teaching, Miller says, is to watch his students go on to make significant contributions to the scientific understanding of behavior. A young colleague of his sums up Miller's success as a teacher in tongue-in-cheek behavioral jargon: "Dr. Miller has been consistently reinforced for making unreasonable demands on his students."

• • • •

Miss Bielski was comatose for almost a month. Her first vague memories following the operation are of nurses asking her to sit up in bed. She remembers cursing them for disturbing her. Over the next few days, she gradually became more alert and cooperative, and, little by little, with the aid of a physiotherapist, she began to regain some control of the muscles on her left side. But most of her waking hours were spent in a wheelchair, and she was forced to wear an eyepatch because of a persistent palsy in her left eye. When it became clear that more intensive therapy was needed, arrangements were made to transfer her to the Institute of Rehabilitation Medicine at New York University Medical Center. But there was no opening for her until late in June, and Miss Bielski was able to convince the doctors that instead of staying at the hospital, where, she felt, she was simply "wasting insurance benefits," she could just as easily wait at home, where her mother could take care of her. On May 28 she was discharged and went home to the fifth-floor walkup. An enormous relief at being out of "hospital white" soon gave way to a more realistic appraisal of the situation, and by the end of her second week at home Miss Bielski realized that she had made a mistake. She felt trapped in the apartment, which was hot and muggy; living with her mother again after eight years on her own was a difficult adjustment; and she was forced to admit that she was "a lot sicker" than she had thought. Tired, weak, constantly dizzy, she somehow managed to get through the month, and on June 22 she was admitted to the Institute of Rehabilitation Medicine. Her blood pressure, which had remained within acceptable limits in the first few weeks after the operation, was now up to 180/100 and, instead of stabilizing after her admission to the Institute, it continued to rise. A normal blood-pressure reading is somewhere around 120/70. When Miss Bielski's pressure reached 230/140, she was rushed around the corner to the Medical Center's University Hospital, where she was put on tranquilizers, a diuretic, and a high dosage of an anti-hypertension drug dispensed under the brand name Aldomet. Within a week her blood pressure was in the 150/100 range—still high but not immediately dangerous —and she was able to return to the Institute, with the notation on her record "Blood pressure under control with Diuril and Aldomet."

The goal of all science, as Miller sees it, is to account for the greatest number of facts with the fewest possible assumptions, in conformity with what is sometimes referred to as the Law of Parsimony. Philosophers know it as Ockham's razor: "Entities must not be unnecessarily multiplied," or, in layman's language: "Never accept a complicated explanation where a simpler one will do." Learning theory is an attempt to set down in one parsimonious package some of the regularities of behavior that experimental psychologists have observed in their laboratories over the years. Like the laws of physics, the laws of learning can be expressed in either prescriptive or statistical language, and they can be useful in comprehending situations far removed from the original laboratory context. Some of the laws seem to be nothing but elaborate paraphrases of common sense. To anyone who knows what a habit is, for instance, it will hardly come as a revelation that consistently rewarded behavior tends to be repeated. But other laws contradict what everyone "knows" from personal experience. According to learning theory, steady practice in itself will *not* lead to the strengthening of learned behavior. Just the opposite—there is no quicker way to extinguish a learned skill or habit than to practice it steadily in the absence of continued reinforcement. Most behaviorists even lean toward the view that there is no such thing as forgetting in the conventional sense. What appears to be the decay of certain memory traces with the passage of time may be an active weeding out, or unlearning, of stimulus-response connections that interfere with connections providing a higher payoff.

Most of the laws of learning were first worked out in carefully controlled experiments with white rats and other laboratory animals and then tested and confirmed with human subjects. The rationale for this procedure can be found in a key hypothesis of experimental psychology. In Miller's words, "all the psychological processes found in other mammals are likely also to be present in man." Some justification for this assumption comes from studies in comparative anatomy indicating that man's vertebrate ancestors built up a bigger and better nervous system through a process of accretion. New neural structures, instead of replacing the old, were literally piled on top of one another, culminating in the twin cerebral hemispheres that cap the human brain stem and spinal cord. As far as brain structure is concerned, rats and men have much in common—up to a point. The most distinctive part of the human brain is the neocortex, the layer of gray cells that covers the surface of the cerebral hemispheres. Man's greatly enlarged cortex is capable of processing far more information and organizing far more complicated tasks than the brain of any other animal, but from the anatomical evidence alone there is no way of knowing how closely the new cortical functions are related to the "old Adam" below. Does man behave like a lower-order mammal in certain ways and like a self-aware rational being in others? Is he literally divided against himself? Or can one coherent set of principles be found to account for the entire spectrum of human behavior, from the most primitive responses to the most advanced—from the reflex sneeze of the newborn infant to the abstract cognition of the poet or the mathematician?

Numerous attempts have been made to bring the same degree of order to the behavioral spectrum that the laws of physics brought to electromagnetism, but none of the proposed theories have won wide acceptance among experimental psychologists. Instead, over the years most researchers have settled for a less parsimonious explanation of the peculiarities of human nature. By postulating one or more radical jumps in the long chain of evolution leading to man, they feel justified in assigning radically different laws to the "lower" and "higher" levels of behavior. Not all psychologists divide the spectrum in exactly the same place or for exactly the same reasons. But there is near unanimity about the category of behavior that belongs at the bottom of the scale. In colloquial usage, the phrase "visceral reaction," or "gut reaction," refers to an automatic, unthinking, and therefore irremediably primitive response of the individual to his environment. It would be no exaggeration to say that this usage has been firmly endorsed by the modern life sciences. The great neuroanatomists of the nineteenth and early twentieth centuries set out to map the structure of the entire nervous system. They succeeded in laying bare the pathways that make up the so-called somatic nervous system, which provides a direct link between individual skeletal muscles and the higher brain centers. But the neural circuitry serving the internal organs and glands presented a different and more confusing picture. These organs and glands seemed to be linked to the higher brain centers only indirectly, through a series of ganglia, which one early researcher likened to a chain of "little brains." While the anatomical evidence was far from conclusive—considering the technical difficulties of the research involved—it happened to fit in with an already prevalent view that the viscera belonged to a lower, more primitive level of organization. For the moment, it seemed both logical and practical to treat this lower level as a separate entity—a bit of the "old Adam" that had somehow retained its autonomy when the higher brain centers were superimposed on it during a later stage of human evolution.

More recent research has shown that elaborate avenues of communication exist between the somatic network and the autonomic one. Yet modern textbooks continue to draw a sharp distinction between the two, and many psychologists have found it convenient to divide the behavioral spectrum along similar lines. As Miller puts it, a number of traditional beliefs have "coalesced" into an assertion that instrumental learning is possible only with those responses which are under the control of the somatic nervous system. The reasoning behind this assertion is not hard to follow. Every healthy member of every species enters life with a vast repertoire of unlearned stimulus-response connections, which produces what is known as instinctive behavior. No one has to teach a newborn infant to cry, or to suck a nipple, or to close his fingers around an object thrust into his palm. Crying, sucking, and grasping are all innate reflexes—behavioral patterns wired into the nervous system and ready to be triggered into action by appropriate stimuli. Many reflexes—sucking, for one—have been observed in the human fetus. Others appear within the first few weeks after birth. Still others, like those having to do with reproduction, may not become operative until the organism matures. A simple reflex, such as the eye-blink that follows a touch on the cornea, may guard the organism against danger from the outside world. Reflexes may also be chained together in elaborate relays and feedback loops to help maintain optimal conditions within the body—the stable internal environment that the physiologist calls "homeostasis" and the layman calls "good health." Yet, no matter how varied the built-in repertoire, innate reflexes are based on stereotyped responses to predictable stimuli. And since the world keeps changing, the organism that is capable of modifying at least some of its behavioral units in the light of its own experience—that is, through instrumental learning—will have a greater chance of survival. Flexibility of this kind is the hallmark of most skeletal behavior. (The rat learns to press a lever with its paw to get a pellet of food; the infant learns to reach out for a teething ring; the racing-car driver learns to control his vehicle with a precision far beyond that attained by the average motorist.) But both science and common sense have long maintained that there is no room for instrumental learning in the blind interplay of visceral reflexes. By and large, homeostasis is maintained by involuntary, unconscious mechanisms, and when outside stimuli do interfere with these mechanisms the glands and internal organs seem to respond only in stereotyped patterns associated with strong emotion or psychosomatic illness: the blush of the shy lover, the intestinal spasm of the terrified soldier, the high blood pressure of the harried executive. It is usually taken for granted that the higher brain centers cannot alter such behavior except by the most indirect means: the frightened soldier can pray for courage or get drunk or remove himself from the battlefield, but he cannot simply turn off an intestinal spasm at will, the way he might raise or lower his arm. It is even possible to argue that a sharp break between the visceral functions and the cerebral control centers is a *necessary* biological development. In contrast to the endless flexibility of skeletal responses, the survival value of emotional behavior becomes apparent only when large numbers of visceral responses fire together—as in the familiar fear-alarm reaction that prepares an organism for a burst of instrumental activity. The release of adrenalin into the bloodstream at such moments is just one part of a general mobilization of bodily resources that is often described as "the flight-or-fight syndrome." According to the traditional argument, while an individual might occasionally find it convenient to exert voluntary control over a specific visceral organ, the frequent exercise of such control could seriously upset the homeostatic balance of the organism and so make it more vulnerable to outside dangers.

Of course, no amount of speculation about evolution could ever prove visceral learning to be impossible. But the arguments against it seemed so persuasive for so long that the great majority of behavioral scientists were effectively discouraged from looking into the matter more deeply.

• • • •

In the third week of July, Miss Bielski's personal physician came to visit her at the Institute of Rehabilitation Medicine. In the course of his visit he told her that, even with the drugs she was taking, her blood pressure was still too high. He also told her about a new experimental method of teaching people to control their own blood pressure. He said that the scientists who had developed the method happened to be conducting tests on volunteers at University Hospital, and he thought she might be a good candidate for the experiment. As he talked, Miss Bielski realized for the first time that her high blood pressure had probably had something to do with her brain hemorrhage.

Primary hypertension has been described by one authority as "a disease of biological regulation dependent upon a complex mosaic of individual and interacting anatomical, biochemical, and nervous-system mechanisms." Physicians know it as chronic high blood pressure without any clear organic cause. In the normal blood-pressure cycle, which is repeated about seventy-two times a minute, the left ventricle of the heart fills with freshly oxygenated blood from the lungs and then contracts like a bellows, forcing its contents through a narrow opening into the aorta. As a result of this contraction, or systole, of the heart, the pressure of the blood against the walls of the arteries quickly reaches a peak, which is sufficient to raise a column of mercury in a glass tube to a height of between 100 and 140 millimeters. Less than half a second later, during the relaxation, or diastole, of the heart, the pressure in the arterial system falls to its lowest level; this diastolic pressure normally ranges between 60 and 90 millimeters. When the admitting physician at the Institute of Rehabilitation Medicine wrote "B.P. 180/100" on Miss Bielski's chart, he was recording a systolic pressure of 180 millimeters and a diastolic pressure of 100. An abnormally high systolic pressure may not be by itself medically significant. The best indicator of danger is the diastolic reading, which in the typical case of hypertension remains above a hundred on repeated examinations. Even with such consistently high pressure, the hypertensive person experiences no physical disability at first; in fact, he may not become aware of his condition for several years unless it is diagnosed during a routine physical checkup or on a visit to the doctor's office for some other complaint. Sooner or later, though, the strain on the cardiovascular system begins to show, with serious complications involving the brain, the heart, the eyes, or the kidneys. Since the exact cause of hypertension is not understood (emotional stress seems to be implicated, but no one knows just how), the standard treatment is strictly symptomatic. There are a number of drugs that are effective in lowering the pressure. But the drugs often have unfortunate side effects, among them fainting, mental depression, changes in the blood count, and allergic reactions such as rashes and fever, and, even apart from these drawbacks, some physicians doubt their long-range efficacy.

In the last week of July, Dr. Miller's research associate Barry Dworkin interviewed Miss Bielski. He came away with the impression that she was an ideal subject for the blood-pressure experiments. She was young, she was strongly motivated to get well, and she was neither too busy nor too sick to participate in frequent and lengthy training sessions. She was also bright, verbal, and cooperative—exactly the kind of person Dworkin felt he could work comfortably with on a day-to-day basis. Miss Bielski, for her part, remembers that Dworkin was "very assertive"—which she liked—and was one of the few people she had met in the hospital "who didn't treat all patients as if they had an IQ of three."

Both her personal physician and the doctor in charge of her physiotherapy agreed that her participation in the blood-pressure experiment could not do her any harm, and that it probably offered the best hope for lengthening her life. Miss Bielski said later, "I believed them. I had to believe them. There didn't seem to be anything else."

• • • •

Miller's long-range program to teach rats and people to control their glands and internal organs was highly unorthodox in many ways, but his experimental strategy was solidly based on conventional learning theory and on the simple biological fact that the body's vital functions are never maintained at a perfectly constant level. Even when the organism is at rest, slight fluctuations occur from moment to moment in the heart rate, the body temperature, the diastolic blood pressure, and so forth. These spontaneous increases and decreases are normally of no significance, since they tend to cancel each other out, leaving a relatively stable baseline. But Miller reasoned that if certain fluctuations could be treated as responses and reinforced appropriately, learning would take place; for instance, if every decrease in diastolic pressure was rewarded, the baseline of the blood-pressure cycle would gradually shift downward as the organism tried to earn more and more rewards.

The key to success in instrumental training is knowing exactly when to reinforce and—equally important—when not to, and making this split-second decision can be difficult even with the more accessible skeletal responses. With a deeply buried visceral function like blood pressure, the technical problems proved to be of another order of magnitude entirely. To begin with, the monitoring system had to be absolutely safe and virtually painless, and it had to provide absolutely reliable feedback within a fraction of a second, because a reward delivered after even the slightest upward movement in diastolic pressure would act as a reward for increasing pressure, and a few such contradictory lessons could undermine the entire training program. Since the only known method of measuring blood pressure on a moment-to-moment basis involved the rather drastic means of placing a needle into an artery, Dworkin had to design and build a completely new system, working in collaboration with Miller and with Dr. Saran Jonas, an associate professor of clinical neurology at the New York University School of Medicine. The basic components included an inflatable pressure cuff; a servopump (to keep the cuff at the proper pressure); an oscilloscope and a polygraph machine (for recording all the data); and a panel of programing circuits, to regulate the rest of the apparatus. The first series of tests was conducted at Rockefeller University, using both healthy volunteers and people with mild hypertension. The results were so encouraging that the researchers decided to shift their base of operations to University Hospital, where, it was assumed, a pool of suitable hypertensive subjects would be available.

A typical training session lasted about an hour. The subject lay face up on a cot in a quiet, darkened room with the inflatable pressure cuff wrapped around his arm at the biceps, where the brachial artery—the major artery in the upper arm—runs close to the skin. Instead of a physician's stethoscope, a small microphone had been placed inside the cuff to pick up the sounds of blood pulsing through the partly constricted artery. Any physician could have translated these sounds into an approximate blood-pressure reading, but Dworkin's machine tracked the subject's diastolic pressure on a heartbeat-to-heartbeat basis—something that no physician could conceivably do. In addition, the machine monitored other vital functions, such as heart rate and respiration, through several small electrodes taped to different parts of the body; the signals from these electrodes were fed into separate channels of the polygraph, and a permanent record of the subject's internal behavior was traced in black ink on a roll of graph paper directly in front of the operator of the machine (but out of sight of the subject himself).

The basic strategy was to reward the subject whenever his diastolic pressure dropped to a level that had been arbitrarily selected as a criterion of therapeutic progress. The reward was nothing but an electronic tone that came on automatically to inform the subject that he was making the correct response. (To a sick person who desperately wants to get well, any indication of improvement, however small or transitory, should be an effective reinforcement.) Although each subject was told in advance that he was going to learn to lower his blood pressure, his only specific instructions at the start of the session were "Lie still, relax, and try to keep the tone on." The difficulty of this assignment depended entirely on the setting of the criterion. For example, the initial criterion might be set just below the subject's current baseline, so that a spontaneous drop of a millimeter or two would trigger a reinforcing tone. If the subject stayed below that setting for a while, the operator simply turned a knob to lower the criterion by four or five millimeters—which automatically shut off the tone until the subject's pressure fell to the new setting. While "chasing the tone" in this way, a few subjects managed to reduce their diastolic pressure by as much as fifteen millimeters in an hour. Since the heart rate remained unchanged, it looked as if the subjects had actually learned to control the reflex mechanisms responsible for dilating the miles and miles of blood vessels in the circulatory system.

The subjects themselves found it hard to accept the fact that anything so important could be accomplished without the direction, or even the knowledge, of their conscious minds. Perhaps because breathing is an internal function that can be controlled voluntarily, most of the subjects started adjusting their respiratory rate in order to improve their performance. Slow, deep, evenly spaced breathing seemed to be the most popular maneuver, but the polygraph record indicated that this had no more than a transitory effect on blood pressure. The subjects also tried to control their pressure through mental discipline of one kind or another. A few made an effort to think only calm, pleasant thoughts; others concentrated on listening to the tone and nothing else; still others tried to empty their minds of all thoughts and sensations, so that their bodies could take over. No one could say for sure whether such efforts had any influence on the learning process. One thing soon became clear, however: The dramatic reductions in blood pressure achieved in the early sessions were disappointingly short-lived, and it was impossible to prove that the gradually declining baselines exhibited by some of the patients were not simply due to a "placebo effect"—a lessening of physical and mental tensions brought about by exposure to the experimental situation itself. The typical hypertensive subject whose diastolic reading dropped from 130 millimeters to 115 in a single hour on the cot would return a day or two later for his next session with a reading of 130, and he would repeat this sequence day after day without any lasting benefit. It was as if he had to relearn the lesson from scratch each time. Conceivably, the trouble lay in the fact that the subject's newly acquired control of his blood pressure was totally dependent on the feedback provided by the tone; as soon as the subject was unhooked from the machine, all possibility of selective reinforcement ceased. But since the upward and downward fluctuations in his diastolic pressure did not cease, this meant that he was performing the correct response thousands of times a day without further reinforcement. The outcome was quite predictable, according to learning theory. The subject's control was bound to keep fading (or "extinguishing," as the behaviorists say) unless some way could be found to monitor his blood pressure and provide suitable rewards *between* sessions. Since a portable version of Dworkin's cumbersome machine would not be feasible for a long time, one logical alternative was to try to teach the subjects to become more aware of increases and decreases on their own. With this additional skill, they might be able to cue themselves into a therapeutic response whenever their control started to fade, and reward themselves with the awareness of a job well done when their pressure returned to normal.

• • • •

On August 4, when Miss Bielski was wheeled through the corridors of University Hospital to her first lesson in blood-pressure control, she was still receiving large doses of anti-hypertensive medication. During July her blood pressure had been read three times a day by nurses on her ward; her mean diastolic reading for the month was 97, with occasional excursions as high as 130. The initial training procedure that Dworkin and Miller had worked out for her was slightly different from the approach they had used in the earlier clinical tests. Instead of a continuous tone, Miss Bielski heard only a single "beep" whenever she passed a criterion. To get further reinforcement, she had to improve her performance. Sometimes, instead of asking her to lower her pressure, Dworkin would instruct her to increase it, or to hold it steady, or to make it go up and down like a yo-yo. Whenever she responded correctly to these instructions, she received an immediate beep of approval.

And in between beeps Dworkin tried to keep talking to her, informing her when her pressure was approaching a criterion, when she was slipping back a bit, when she was doing particularly well, when her responses seemed unusually sluggish. The idea behind the altered training procedure was not only to establish a control for a placebo effect but also to supply her with more detailed feedback about her cardiovascular responses and encourage her to pay more attention to what was actually happening inside her body.

After two weeks of intensive training, a general declining trend in diastolic pressure was observed. By the middle of September, Miss Bielski's pressure was down as low as 70. The researchers were elated. But since the patient was still taking Aldomet and Diuril, it was difficult to say how much of the decrease was due to the cumulative effect of the drugs and how much to the training. On September 15, at the request of the researchers and with the approval of her physician, the Aldomet was withdrawn. The next day Miss Bielski's pressure began to climb. By September 20, her diastolic was up to 92, and the doctors had begun to talk about putting her back on Aldomet. But during the next day's session her pressure fell again, to 87; the day after that it was down to 77. Apparently it had taken Miss Bielski a few days to learn to compensate for the extra load when the medication was suddenly withdrawn. Now she appeared to be in control again.

A more severe test lay just ahead. Even without medication, some hypertensive patients show a spontaneous improvement in a hospital environment, only to have their pressure shoot up as soon as they return home. Miss Bielski had rented a new apartment in a large elevator building directly across the street from University Hospital; she intended to live alone there and commute daily by wheelchair to her training-and-therapy sessions in the Medical Center. On Friday, September 25, she made the move. Over the weekend she was aware of great anxiety in trying to cope with the outside world. Aside from the challenge of getting her apartment in shape, she had to get used to the everyday problems of bathing and dressing and feeding herself, and of having no one available at a moment's notice in case she needed help. On Monday her diastolic pressure had risen to 90. The research team prepared for the worst. But the next day her diastolic reading dropped to 79, and over the next two weeks, while she was getting accustomed to the stresses and strains of her new life, her diastolic level remained in the high seventies and low eighties. Miss Bielski and her instructors breathed a little easier.

•   •   •   •

Miller is one of a handful of experimental psychologists who have argued consistently (his colleagues might even say stubbornly) for what is known as a "global" view of man. He has always proceeded on the assumption that human behavior is all of a piece; that all responses to the environment, whether on a visceral or skeletal or cognitive level, are governed by the same basic laws—the laws of instrumental learning—and that the key to this unity is the continuous, multileveled integrative function performed by the human brain, which he once referred to, in an uncharacteristic burst of rhetoric, as the "greatest miracle in the universe."

"We no longer view the brain as merely an enormously complicated telephone switchboard, which is passive unless excited from without," Miller said on another occasion (his installation as president of the American Psychological Association for the 1960–1961 term). "The brain is a device for sorting, processing, and analyzing information. The brain contains sense organs which respond to states of the internal environment, such as osmotic pressure, temperature, and many others. The brain is a gland which secretes chemical messengers, and it also responds to such messengers, as well as to various types of feedback, both central and peripheral. A combination of behavioral and physiological techniques is increasing our understanding of these processes and their significance for psychology."

Almost a decade later, in a progress report on visceral learning published in the issue of *Science* for January 31, 1969, Miller took to task the legions of behavioral scientists who, without seriously investigating the matter, had simply assumed that instrumental learning on the visceral level was impossible. Looking over the evidence usually cited in support of this view, he could find nothing but "two incompletely reported exploratory experiments and a vague allusion to the Russian literature," and he concluded, "It is only against a cultural background of great prejudice that such weak evidence could lead to such a strong conviction." In Western culture, he wrote, the prejudice goes back at least as far as Plato's "invidious dichotomy" between the higher, rational soul in the head and the lower, appetitive souls in the body. "Since ancient times, reason and the voluntary responses of the skeletal muscles have been considered to be superior, while emotions and the presumably involuntary glandular and visceral responses have been considered to be inferior."

Scientists are obviously not immune to general cultural prejudices. But their experience in framing, testing, and, if necessary, discarding hypotheses makes it easier for them to accept the possibility that long-unchallenged habits of thought might be wrong. And, because of the great influence of science on contemporary thought, the laboratory demonstration of visceral learning can be expected to produce intellectual tremors far beyond its immediate range of application. On one level, the visceral-learning experiments directly challenge the assumptions that lie behind Western man's profound alienation from his own body. On another level, the work of Miller and other researchers in this field opens the door for a fresh look at some of the so-called higher mental processes, like consciousness and volition, which have up to now resisted a satisfactory behavioral formulation.

•   •   •   •

The high point of Miss Bielski's blood-pressure training came during a session one day in the middle of October:

10 A.M.: Miss Bielski arrives and is hooked up to the machine.

10:15: Her pressure is tracked for one minute to get a reliable baseline reading. Mean diastolic pressure during that minute is 76.

10:20: First trial. The training cuff around her left arm is inflated. Dworkin tells her to try to increase pressure. One minute later, her pressure has risen to 94. Dworkin says, "Fine," and the cuff is deflated.

10:25: After a brief rest, the cuff is reinflated. "Let's try to decrease now," Dworkin says. One minute later, her pressure is down to 72. "Very good," Dworkin says. "Now hold it there." One minute later, her pressure is 73. The cuff is deflated.

10:30: Second trial. Instructions to decrease. After two minutes, her pressure is 74. The cuff is deflated.

10:40: Third trial. Instructions to decrease. After one minute, pressure is down to 66. After two minutes, pressure stands at 65. "Excellent," Dworkin says. The cuff is deflated.

Net change during session: 29 millimeters (ranging from a high of 94 to a low of 65).

Conventional English usage tells us that our behavior is "voluntary" when we are doing what we intend to do and "conscious" when we are fully aware of what we are doing. A moment's introspection, together with some minimal knowledge of physiology, however, reveals that nothing we do ever comes close to meeting these criteria. The behavior we call voluntary and conscious actually depends on a substratum of reflex actions, most of which—like the barrage of neural signals to and from the brain, the simultaneous flexing and relaxing of dozens of muscles, the intricate metabolic adjustments—occur without causing the slightest subjectively perceived sensation. This is not to say that there are no objective differences between the peristaltic contractions of a newborn baby's intestines and the exquisitely orchestrated finger movements of a neurosurgeon at work. But Miller argues that our efforts to comprehend these differences have been hampered by an uncritical acceptance of "folklore" categories such as conscious/unconscious and voluntary/involuntary. "Just because we have certain word pairs in our language doesn't mean that they necessarily represent the best way to slice reality," he has said. "We may be dealing with what I call Monday-Tuesday-Wednesday definitions. If you define all the different things that happen on those days as Monday-things, Tuesday-things, and Wednesday-things, your definitions will be accurate as far as they go, but they won't help you much in understanding the events themselves." For Miller, the discovery of visceral learning—which cuts across all the existing categories—only emphasizes the confusion inherent in our traditional view of the higher mental processes. "Suppose I were to tell you that I'd achieved complete voluntary control of my ear-wiggling response," he says. "How would you go about verifying this statement? You'd probably begin by asking me to wiggle both ears, then just the right ear, then just the left. The acid test would be whether or not I could follow your instructions to the letter." In conventional terminology, with its subjective bias, the paradox is inescapable: To prove that his behavior is voluntary, a person must be able to respond on cue as if he had no free will at all. However, the confusion disappears if such responses are defined *operationally.* From an objective point of view, voluntary behavior is simply behavior that has been brought under the control of a special kind of stimulus—a stimulus with symbolic content, which is usually, but not necessarily, a verbal cue. As Miller puts it, "When we set out to make blood pressure voluntary, our task is done if we can arrange it so that whenever we say, 'Decrease,' the subject's pressure goes down, and whenever we say, 'Increase,' the subject's pressure goes up." By the same logic, blood-pressure control can be defined as "conscious" if the subject, in responding to instructions, can accurately report the changes that are occurring inside his body, and guide his subsequent responses accordingly.

The whole purpose of an operational definition is to pin down an elusive, hard-to-measure variable in terms of a more accessible phenomenon. Weather conditions, for example, are usually defined in terms of the behavior of certain instruments—thermometer, barometer, hygrometer. Although these instruments do not provide an exhaustive description of the weather, they give a picture that is detailed enough for most purposes. To the layman's eye, however, Miller's operational definition of "conscious control" seems to ignore precisely that detail which most people consider to be the essence of human consciousness. Our personal experience, supported by a cultural heritage of several millennia, assures us that somewhere inside the person seen by others there is an invisible core of being— a purely private self that observes, if it cannot always control, our public actions and is ultimately free of all controls imposed on the organism from outside. Whether it makes any sense or not, that is what it *feels* like to be conscious, and any definition of "conscious control" that fails to mention such a feeling is like a weather report that fails to mention whether it is raining or sunny.

Miller concedes that there is almost certainly more to human consciousness than the ability to respond to and manipulate symbolic cues. "I'm not sure how to describe it, but there seems to be some kind of multi-sensory, total-field experience that helps us organize our most complex and flexible behavior." Yet this is still a far cry from the notion of an autonomous individual inside the behaving organism—a notion that Miller, as a behaviorist, cannot accept. In fact, he argues that the conscious control of behavior is itself a product of the gradual socialization of the human infant through instrumental conditioning. As a working hypothesis, Miller has assumed that the superiority of man's mental powers over those of his animal forebears can be explained without postulating any radically new behavioral principles. In his view, the really significant factors are man's innate ability to use symbolic cues and the possession of a much greater information-processing capacity. While the laws governing reinforcement presumably remain the same from rat to man, the superior resources available in the human nervous system make possible an incomparably greater flexibility in reinforcement schedules. This means, among other things, that a response can now be modified *before* it occurs through anticipated rewards and punishments. Miller points out that since symbols are created and transmitted by men in society, symbolic control of a response actually implies a kind of social control. At the same time, the use of symbolic cues places a premium on the ability of the organism to become conscious of its own responses. As Miller notes, there are only two visceral functions that are routinely subjected to socially determined schedules of reinforcement—urination and defecation—and these are the only visceral functions that are routinely brought under voluntary and conscious control. "The analysis may be somewhat oversimplified," Miller says, "but perhaps we can say that the average person does not have any specificity of feelings from the viscera because he hasn't learned the right labels for them, and perhaps he doesn't have the right labels because most visceral functions are not normally observed by other people, and so are not normally brought under social control. In other words, it may be that we are not conscious of these sensations *only* because we have not been trained to label them."

•　•　•　•

During the ten-week period in which Miss Bielski achieved the greatest control of her blood pressure, she wrote down some of her impressions about the learning process in the form of an essay.

> I was determined to succeed [she reported]. I felt that this was the only part of my treatment that I could do anything about at all, and I am a habitual overachiever. At first, it seemed that lowering my pressure was only a simple muscular trick. I thought it was a matter of relaxing my stomach, my chest, my breathing, but none of these worked all the time. I found I could drop my pressure quickly by fooling with my muscles, but I could only sustain the drop if I "relaxed" my mind. It all seemed to depend on clearing my mind of all stressful thoughts. It's almost the yoga thing, almost self-hypnosis. Usually, when I'm on the cot, I try to think of my brain as a lake inside my head. Once, I tried to think about lying on the beach, but that was too stimulating. Making the pressure go up is a lot easier than lowering it. The best way to get it up is to take

a big breath and think angry thoughts—I may remember some real jackass I knew in the past, and get mad all over again at his stupidity. But any kind of mental effort, even adding a lot of big numbers, seems to have a similar effect.

One thing I've noticed in trying to keep my pressure down is that it's no good trying to think *phony* comforting thoughts. I mean, if I start getting tense about having to cross First Avenue in my wheelchair with all that heavy traffic and a short green light, I can't just tell myself, "Oh, First Avenue is really a cinch," because it isn't, and I *know* it isn't. But what I can do is remind myself that I can get plenty of help to cross the street if I need it, and this usually works, because it's comforting and also *true*.

If I pay very close attention, I think I can tell when my pressure is up or down, but I can't always hold it there smoothly. What I mean is, when I'm trying to lower it, I know sometimes it goes up and I can detect the change, but my lowering maneuver takes several seconds to work. I'm not sure why this happens. There seems to be some sort of vibration inside my head when my pressure is high. One day just before I left the hospital, I was conscious of the blood rushing through my arteries. I could tell my pressure was high and it frightened me a little, so I called for a nurse. She took it, and it was 112, which was way above normal for me at that time. So I tried to lower it with the techniques I'd learned, and then I asked her to take it again, and it was down to 90.

I always depend very heavily on Barry Dworkin's encouragement and on his personality. I think he could be an Olympic coach. He not only seems aware of my general condition but he is never satisfied with less than my best, and I can't fool him. I feel we are friends and allies—it's really as though *we* were lowering my pressure.

•   •   •   •

Having spent more than a decade investigating a phenomenon that most of his colleagues were convinced did not exist, Miller now tends to be wary of the current public interest in visceral learning and in other medical applications of what has recently been called "biofeedback training." The danger he anticipates is that, as he said recently, "overoptimistic publicity will arouse impossible hopes for quick miracle cures, which will, in turn, lead to premature disillusionment with the whole approach." Characteristically, he counsels long-range optimism combined with extreme caution about the immediate future. And he offers in evidence the continuing case history of Robin Bielski.

The facts are briefly stated: After achieving what appeared to be a remarkable degree of voluntary, and even conscious, control over her blood pressure, Miss Bielski suffered a severe setback. A number of personal experiences brought home to her—apparently for the first time —the true extent of her physical handicaps and forced her to realize just how difficult it was going to be to resume what she considered a normal life in the city. On top of this discovery, she was told that she would have to undergo a delicate operation to correct a squint in her left eye. Miss Bielski's reaction was predictable: Her blood pressure started to rise. At this critical point her entire rehabilitation and training program was interrupted for two weeks while she and a friend went on a Caribbean cruise that she had been looking forward to for some time. Her doctors had decided that the change would be good for her morale, but to be on the safe side they prescribed a supply of Diuril and Aldomet for the trip. When she returned, her diastolic pressure was in the 90-to-100 range. She has taken anti-hypertensive medication ever since, and her response to further visceral training—conducted not by Dworkin but by a colleague whom he taught to use the apparatus—was poor.

Clearly, visceral training had little or no lasting therapeutic effect in Miss Bielski's case. But what is not yet clear is whether she lost *all* voluntary control of her blood pressure or whether her control was simply not strong enough to overcome the effects of the constant stress she was subjected to for several months. (The fact that a man collapses under the burden of a 500-pound weight does not prove that he cannot lift a 200-pound weight.) Of course, there is a third possibility—that Miss Bielski never really achieved any voluntary control at all. Miller concedes that there is no way to prove that the general declining trend in the subject's pressure over the course of her training was not merely a placebo effect, "based on the hope of cure that was held out to her, plus the impressiveness of the apparatus and her personal relationship with the experimenter." But he goes on to say that he cannot imagine how such factors could ever account for the subject's "uncanny ability to make her pressure go either up or down on command," and he and Dworkin hope to teach her to regain this control, in a new series of experiments.

It remains to be seen whether any other subjects can be taught to raise or lower their pressure with the degree of success that Miss Bielski once enjoyed. For the moment, Miller hesitates to draw any firm conclusions from one possibly atypical case. "The whole business is much more complicated than that," he says. "For instance, even if our theory is perfectly correct we might still run into a situation where a patient is getting some specific benefit from a particular symptom and does not *want* to give it up. We're settling down now to the long and difficult task of determining exactly what the important variables are, and trying out new techniques—one by one—to overcome the obstacles we have already encountered."

When a research project reaches this frustrating stage, even as single-minded a scientist as Miller may feel the need for a little positive feedback to reassure him that he is still on the right track. The informal experiment in ear-wiggling served this purpose. After nearly a year of intermittent practice, Miller finally satisfied his own criterion of success: he learned to wiggle his right ear at will. In keeping with his standard operating procedure, he experimented with a number of different approaches to the problem. One approach called for him to focus his attention on the sensations on both sides of his face while he wiggled his ears, and then to try to imagine these sensations occurring on the right side only. He also tried to imagine the left side of his face as cold or numb, so that the ear on that side would be unable to wiggle. Miller was not very surprised when neither of these techniques worked. Nor did he expect to have much success simply willing a specific response into existence. His lifelong study of the learning process had convinced him that the only way to build a new physical habit was to take an already existing neural connection between brain and muscle and bring it under specific stimulus control through differential reinforcement. "I may have been prejudiced because it fitted in so well with my theory, but I found that the best technique was to stand in front of the mirror, where I could see what was happening, and then try to shape the response one small step at a time," Miller told me. "I'd start by trying to produce the most minute independent movement with my right ear. Then I'd try to increase it a little bit each day. If my left ear started to move at any time, I'd drop back until I was sure that only the right one was moving. Then I'd start increasing the movement again, little by little. Eventually . . ." Miller paused, and his face took on a look of intense concentration. His right ear began to twitch against the side of his head. His left ear seemed perfectly motionless. After about thirty seconds, he relaxed and broke into a wide grin. It was obvious that in this small matter, as in all scientific endeavors, success was its own reward.

2

Of Rats and Men

The relationship between fact and theory in creative scientific research is not nearly so straightforward as the general public has been led to believe. The layman usually thinks of a theory as an attempt to make sense out of a mass of accumulated facts, but one function of a scientific theory is to define a problem in objective terms that will permit relevant facts to be gathered. According to Neal Miller, "A theory may be fruitful, leading to valuable research, even though it is eventually proved to be wrong—or, indeed, *because* it is formulated specifically enough so that it can be disproved." The role that mistaken theories often play in advancing human knowledge is an aspect of the scientific method that most scientists do not like to stress—just as they do not like to talk about the importance of such subjective factors as intuition and emotion in determining which theories are dismissed without ever being put to a serious test. Miller once told an international congress of psychologists in Moscow, "Published reports of research are written with the wisdom of hindsight. They leave out the initial blind groping and fumbling to save journal space (and perhaps also to save face), and exclude almost all of those attempts that are abandoned as failures. Therefore, they present a misleading picture, which is far too orderly and simple, of the actual process of trying to extend the frontiers of science into unknown territory." The specific example Miller had in mind was the zigzag line of research and reasoning that culminated in his own laboratory demonstration of visceral learning.

Among his colleagues, Miller's name is closely associated with a specific theory about learning known as the drive-reduction hypothesis. A drive, according to Miller, is any strong stimulus—such as a sharp pain—that goads an organism into action. In a typical learning situation, the organism will run through a variety of responses in trial-and-error fashion as long as the stimulus continues at high intensity. The first response that is followed by a decrease in the intensity of the drive stimulus will be reinforced—which simply means that this response will probably appear much more quickly the next time the organism faces a similar situation. For example, the pain of a headache may lead a person to place cold compresses on his forehead and to lie down in a darkened room. If the headache persists, the person may eventually remember an advertisement he saw for Brand X headache tablet, and he may ask a friend to run down to the drugstore to get some. If his headache goes away shortly after he takes a Brand X tablet, he will probably reach for Brand X as soon as his next headache begins.

To say that reinforcement—and therefore learning—can sometimes result from drive reduction is to state the obvious. But in what Miller calls the strong form of the drive-reduction hypothesis he goes on to suggest that all reinforcement, and therefore all learning, can be attributed to the same mechanism. In other words, there is no such thing as pleasure *per se;* any enjoyment we derive from a pleasant reward such as food or drink is actually the body's way of registering a decrease in pain or discomfort. At first glance, this appears to be a gloomy, not to say perverse, view of human nature. Miller concedes that the strong form of the drive-reduction hypothesis has "a considerably less than 50-per-cent chance of being correct." Yet some of his most important work during the past thirty-five years, including the visceral-learning project, grew out of his efforts to apply drive-reduction principles to specific problems in the laboratory, and he has vigorously defended the hypothesis against its many critics—"if only," he says, "to highlight the obstacles, and infuriate others into devising superior hypotheses and the experimental programs to support them."

Although Miller's basic approach to the mysteries of the nervous system seems to be based on a kind of intellectual puritanism, his life outside the laboratory belies the image. He and his wife, Marion, live in a comfortable five-room apartment in New York, a short walk from Miller's spacious corner office overlooking the East River at Rockefeller University. Part of his heritage from a childhood in the Pacific Northwest—his father was chairman of the Department of Psychology and Education at Western Washington State College, in Bellingham—is an abiding love for the out-of-doors. Miller and his wife get away from the city as often as possible to their weekend house in Guilford, Connecticut, where he raises tomatoes ("because they're so easy") and an especially sweet variety of corn called Illinois Chief. The Millers also own a rustic summer home on a lake in Maine, which they bought in 1961, when Miller was a professor of psychology at Yale. "It's not very practical now, but we haven't been able to bring ourselves to give it up," Miller says. He tries to spend a few weeks there each year with his family, indulging his passion for fishing. "I take along a pile of work in case I get bored—a precaution which insures that I don't get bored."

The Millers have two children, York, who graduated from Harvard in 1972 and is now attending Duke University Medical School, and Sara, a student at the Rochester Institute of Technology, who is interested in weaving and textile design. Miller takes his role as a father very seriously, but he says that he made no special effort to apply the principles of learning theory while raising his family. "I'm sure the general principles do apply, but in my opinion we just don't have a science of child-rearing yet. There's too much ignorance about the important variables to go into human engineering with any confidence. In fact, my children taught me more about the complexities of human motivation than anything I taught them."

The Miller household has always included pets of some kind. At present Miller and his wife share their apartment with a friendly, shaggy mongrel named Blackie, who was a subject in one of the early visceral-learning experiments at Yale. In those days Miller and his associates borrowed the dogs they needed from the animal pool at the Yale School of Medicine; when the psychologists were through with them, the dogs were returned to the medical school, where they were ultimately used in what medical researchers refer to as acute experiments. "But we liked this one so much," Miller says, "that we decided to save it." Blackie appears to be a perfectly normal dog in every way except for his strange, muted bark—a result of an operation on his vocal cords which was performed on all canine subjects in the laboratory to keep down the noise level.

Like most experimental psychologists, Miller has an attitude of compassion and pragmatism toward the use of animals in scientific research. "You take every precaution to see that they don't suffer unnecessary pain," he says. "But if the study of animal behavior can help alleviate the human suffering caused by physical and mental disorders, I see no alternative. I can respect the point of view of an antivivisectionist—especially if he's also a vegetarian—but, essentially, my sympathies are with human beings." Miller finds an almost perfect expression of his feelings in the technical use of the term "sacrifice," which sometimes appears in scientific papers to describe the killing of an animal to permit a complete anatomical and histological examination. ("After testing, the animal was sacrificed. Its brain was frozen, sectioned, stained, and examined microscopically. . . .")

Through his father, an educational psychologist trained at the University of Chicago by John Dewey and James Rowland Angell, Miller developed an early appreciation of the scientific outlook. He remembers that his father frequently brought home books on general scientific topics and left them lying around the house where a young boy was likely to discover them. But, despite his growing interest in science, Miller was never aware of any pressure to follow in his father's footsteps and only in his senior year at the University of Washington did he decide to major in psychology. After receiving a Bachelor of Science degree in 1931, he went on to take an M.S. at Stanford, where he studied with Lewis Terman. Although Terman is best known as the author of the Stanford-Binet IQ test, he was also interested in theories of personality development, and he expressed strong admiration both for the insights of Sigmund Freud and for the work of Clark L. Hull, professor of psychology at Yale University's Institute of Human Relations. In 1932 Miller went to Yale as a doctoral candidate and was immediately drawn into Hull's orbit.

The purpose of the Institute of Human Relations was to bring together researchers in sociology, psychiatry, anthropology, and experimental psychology to work on important problems that cut across the traditional academic boundaries. Hull's ambition was to create a general theory of behavior sophisticated enough to account for the higher

mental processes and broad enough to unify the two pioneering (and sometimes antagonistic) schools of behavioral
science—one stemming from the work of the Russian
physiologist Ivan P. Pavlov, and the other from the work of
the American psychologist Edward L. Thorndike, who is
credited with the first rigorous investigation of trial-and-
error, or instrumental, learning.

As every high-school student knows, one of the mile-
stones in the history of modern science was Pavlov's
demonstration, early in this century, that a dog can be
conditioned to salivate at the sound of a ringing bell. The
subject in that classic experiment was an animal whose
salivary gland had been attached to a glass tube extending
through its cheek, so that the secretion could be collected
and accurately measured. The dog, immobilized in a
leather harness, was put through a series of training trials.
In each trial, a bell was rung just as meat powder was
applied to the animal's tongue. After a number of close
pairings between the meat powder (which elicits salivation)
and the sound of the bell, the dog began to salivate immediately on hearing the bell, even when the meat powder
was omitted. Pavlov originally called this phenomenon a
psychic reflex, but it soon became known as a conditioned
reflex. He recognized that the phenomenon was worth exploring systematically, and he devoted the rest of his life to
this task. In the vocabulary that Pavlov adopted to describe
his findings, the meat powder was labeled an "unconditioned stimulus" and the bell was labeled a "conditioned
stimulus." Careful research showed that the more frequently the two stimuli were paired in successive training
trials, the stronger the salivary response would be to the
ringing of the bell alone. Conversely, after the conditioned
reflex had been established, repeated ringing of the bell
alone led to a progressive weakening of the response, and
eventually to its extinction—as if the animal had gradually

unlearned the lesson that bell and food went together. Pavlov also noted that a response that had been conditioned to the sound of a particular bell also occurred when bells with slightly different tones were rung, but that the animal could be taught to make a very fine discrimination if the experimenter was careful to reinforce responses to one tone only and to extinguish all responses to other tones.

By one of those strange coincidences in the history of science, Pavlov's work on conditioned reflexes at the turn of the century was paralleled by Thorndike's studies of trial-and-error learning. In a typical experiment performed in his laboratory at Columbia University, Thorndike placed a hungry cat in a puzzle box—a specially designed wooden cage with a latched door that could be opened from the inside if the cat pulled on a loop of string. Outside the door, in full view of the animal, was a dish of food. The cat's first reaction was to go into a frenzy of scratching, biting, and butting at the inside of the cage. In the course of these more or less random responses, the cat eventually swiped at the loop of string with its paw, and the door sprang open. In subsequent trials with the same animal, the period preceding the correct response became shorter and shorter, and the cat's trial-and-error behavior was confined more and more to the general vicinity of the string, until eventually the cat went straight to the string as soon as it was placed in the cage. Thorndike coined the term "law of effect" to describe the gradual strengthening, or reinforcement, of the responses that led to the reward (which in this case included both the food and the chance to escape from confinement).

The most notable difference between the work of Pavlov and that of Thorndike is that Pavlovian conditioning—also known as classical conditioning—is applicable only to responses for which an unconditioned stimulus can be found.

For example, without the use of meat powder (or some equivalent stimulus that normally elicits salivation), Pavlov could never have trained a dog to salivate at the sound of a bell. Similarly, before eye-blinking can be attached to some neutral stimulus, the experimenter must find a stimulus—a jet of air, say—that reliably elicits eye-blinking in the subject. There is no way that meat powder can be used to condition an eye-blink, or a jet of air to condition salivation. By contrast, a researcher using Thorndike's approach and just *one* reward can manipulate virtually any response that the subject is physically capable of.

Despite the obviously greater flexibility of the instrumental techniques pioneered by Thorndike, it was Pavlov's work that became virtually synonymous with behavioral psychology in the popular imagination. This was partly because Pavlov had already formulated a coherent (if controversial) theory to account for his experimental data. But perhaps the most important factor in assuring the dissemination of Pavlovian ideas—in this country, at least—was their adoption by John B. Watson, a professor of psychology at Johns Hopkins University from 1908 to 1920. Watson issued a call as early as 1913 for a completely objective science of behavior, untainted by the sterile attitudes and assumptions of the then dominant school of introspective psychology. Having learned of Pavlov's experiments, probably through reports in French scientific journals, Watson came to the conclusion that even the most complex forms of learned behavior could be built up out of chains of conditioned reflexes—as the most complex molecules are built up out of atoms. Although the English translation of Pavlov's definitive work, *Conditioned Reflexes,* did not appear until 1927, a full decade earlier Watson was proclaiming that the key to the learning process, and therefore the key to all behavior, was already in the hands of the behavioral psychologists. In addition to doing original research with animals and human infants, Watson was an indefatigable propagandist. He joyfully entered into public battle with the old-line introspective psychologists and at the same time took issue with the newfangled Freudians, who had some revolutionary ideas of their own, and who had been receiving a great deal of attention in the popular press since Freud's visit to the United States in 1909. The initial impact of Watson's polemical efforts was extraordinary. When his book *Behaviorism* appeared in 1925, the New York *Herald Tribune* called it "perhaps . . . the most important book ever written," and the *Times* declared, "It marks an epoch in the intellectual history of man."

But it was not long before a reaction set in. Watson's language was often more worthy of the advertising man than of the serious scientist. (In 1920 he was forced to resign his academic post as a result of a divorce scandal, and he did, in fact, pursue a successful career in advertising after that.) Watson defined the goal of psychology as "the prediction and control of behavior," and he spoke as if that goal were well within reach. In *Behaviorism* he wrote:

> Give me a dozen healthy infants, well formed, and my own specified world to bring them up in, and I'll guarantee to take anyone at random and train him to become any type of specialist I might select—doctor, lawyer, artist, merchant-chief, and yes, even beggarman and thief, regardless of his talents, penchants, tendencies, abilities, vocations, and race of his ancestors.

After such a fanfare, even the most impressive achievements of Watson and his followers seemed somehow paltry and beside the point. Their insistence that every response could be reduced to physiological changes in nerves and muscles gained them the reputation of being interested only in "muscle twitches." Even more damaging was the critical line taken by the so-called cognitive theorists, who argued that while a stimulus-response model might be valid for explaining simple physical and emotional reactions, a more sophisticated theory was needed to account for man's rational and creative thought processes. Although the critics of early behaviorism failed to provide a satisfactory alternative theory, it soon became obvious that Watson's original stimulus-response approach was too limited to live up to its advance billing.

During the 1930s and 1940s, the two most influential behavioral scientists in America were Clark Hull and B. F. Skinner. Skinner honed Thorndike's law of effect into a precision tool for the control of behavior. Skinner placed his emphasis on the variables that affect the subject's rate of response. For example, to show how an animal's apparently random responses can be shaped into the most complicated performances, he devised a dramatic classroom presentation involving an untrained pigeon in a confined space and a food-dispenser. In a recent conversation with an interviewer, Skinner described this experiment:

> I ask the class what they want to see the pigeon do—within reason, of course—and in a matter of minutes the pigeon is pacing a figure eight, or bowing to the audience, or what have you. It is a simple matter of operating the food-dispenser at the right time. You can't wait for the pigeon to pace a figure eight before you reinforce it; you'd wait forever. You choose any response which will contribute to that figure eight. You select from available responses any which will lead to the response you are to produce.

The persistence of a learned response is also a function of the schedule of reinforcement, as Skinner has demonstrated:

> If you reinforce every response, then every second response, then every fifth, then every tenth, twenty-fifth, fiftieth, and hundredth, you can get a pigeon to go on indefinitely, re-

sponding one hundred times for each small measure of food. Actually, you can build up to 10,000 responses for each small measure of food. But it takes programing. You can't reach the final stage without going through intervening stages.

Hull's chief contributions to behaviorism were on a more rarefied, theoretical plane. Like Watson, he believed that there were certain regularities of behavior common to all higher organisms and that these could be best described by stimulus-response terminology. In his major theoretical work, *Principles of Behavior,* Hull declared, "For the purposes of analyzing behavior, we have to assume that man is a machine." But there was nothing that said the machine had to be stupid. Hull did not think that learning could be reduced to the simplicity of the conditioned reflex. Rather, he and his students at Yale's Institute of Human Relations saw Pavlovian conditioning as a special case of the broad phenomenon of learning—which Hull described as "the highest and most significant phenomenon produced by the processes of organic evolution."

Pavlov's work had provided experimental psychologists with a useful laboratory tool, but learning theory had to expand its horizons far beyond the conditioned reflex before one could talk about the "prediction and control" of all behavior. In keeping with this general attitude at the Institute, Miller's first project after he received his Ph.D., in 1935, was to examine yet another special case in modern psychology—the clinically oriented work of Sigmund Freud—from the perspective of stimulus-response learning theory. Unfortunately, a couple of serious technical problems stood in Miller's way: first, he didn't know enough about Freud's work; and, second, he didn't have enough money to pursue his studies. "The way you studied psychoanalysis in those days was to be analyzed yourself, preferably by someone at the Vienna Psychoanalytic Institute, or, even better, by Freud himself," Miller explained recently. Although research funds were hard to come by in the middle of the Depression, Miller applied to the Social Science Research Council in Washington and, with the help of his Yale sponsors, received a fellowship to study abroad. This got him to Vienna, but it was not enough to get him onto the Master's couch. Miller still has in his possession two letters (one in German and one in English) in which Dr. Freud expressed interest in the young American's research project but went on to explain that because of his many pressing obligations—specifically, the large number of relatives he had to support—he had been forced to set a minimum fee for his services: a hundred Austrian schillings, or about twenty dollars, per hour of analysis. "If I had known then how many people would ask me what Freud was like, I'd have requested at least one hour's worth just to talk to him," Miller says. "But twenty dollars seemed like too much money at the time." On the Master's personal recommendation, he settled for one of Freud's students, Dr. Heinz Hartmann, who charged much less. (Hartmann later became a well-known analyst in New York.)

Miller considered his eight months of psychoanalysis under Hartmann a highly successful "learning experience." Returning to Yale in the fall of 1936, he entered into a close working relationship with a young sociologist named John Dollard, who had a special interest in the cultural and clinical applications of learning theory. In two major collaborative efforts, *Social Learning and Imitation,* published in 1941, and *Personality and Psychotherapy,* published in 1950, Miller and Dollard tried to show how a sophisticated approach to learning theory could clarify even the most puzzling manifestations of the higher mental processes. To begin with, they defined "stimulus" and "response" in purely operational terms—the operation in this case being the learning process. By so doing, they hoped to extend and deepen the stimulus-response analysis of behavior until it was able to account for virtually any alteration in an organism's internal or external environment—including such elusive mental phenomena as unspoken thoughts, deliberate shifts in attention, ups and downs in such emotional states as fear and anxiety, and even the perception of similarities and discrepancies in spatial patterns or temporal sequences of events.

In any complex living organism, a vast number of stimuli are constantly impinging on a vast number of sensory-nerve endings. The behaviorist, like the animal trainer, is interested primarily in those stimuli, or patterns of stimuli, which become linked in some way with the reinforcement of instrumental responses. For instance, if a stimulus becomes strong enough to galvanize an organism into action, it may be said to function as a drive; a blast of cold air, a headache pain, an electric shock, hunger pangs, sexual desire may all function in this way. Any reduction in the strength of a drive acts as a reward for the immediately preceding behavior—which may be classified as escape responses, eating responses, sexual responses, or whatever. But it is obvious that the behavior of higher organisms cannot be explained solely in terms of drives and rewards. A hungry man is driven to eat, but this does not mean that he will swallow the first object he sees—which may be a box of nails or a black-widow spider. Taking cues from the environment, he will hunt for what he considers to be a suitable source of nourishment. In their first book, Miller and Dollard define a "cue" as any stimulus that is not strong enough to be a drive but that nevertheless helps to determine *when* an organism will respond and *how* it will respond. A cue can be as simple and vivid as the color of a ripe apple hanging on a tree, or it can be as subtle and complicated as the weather conditions that prompt an experienced ship's captain to choose one course rather than another. The success of a response in reducing a drive often depends on the discrimination of reliable cues from a background of "indifferent" stimuli. And such discriminations are themselves responses that can be learned.

With the help of these operational definitions, stimulus-response learning theory had obviously come a long way from "muscle twitches." Indeed, in the opening chapter of *Personality and Psychotherapy* the authors announce that their goal is "to aid in the creation of a psychological base for a general science of human behavior" by bringing together "the three great traditions" of psychoanalysis, experimental psychology, and modern social science. One of the central arguments of the book is that the symptoms of the classic Freudian neuroses can be best understood as instrumental responses learned under conditions of great stress and inner conflict. According to Miller and Dollard, when a person is very fearful or anxious any response that leads to a reduction in fear or anxiety is automatically reinforced and will tend to recur whenever the person feels fearful or anxious again, no matter how inappropriate, or even destructive, the repetition may be in the long run. A neurotic habit formed in this way may be overt, like a temper tantrum or a crying jag, or it may be deeply buried, like the repression of certain thoughts and feelings. In either case, effective psychotherapy may be considered essentially a process of re-education, in which "bad" stimulus-response connections are extinguished and new and "better" responses are attached to the anxiety-provoking stimuli.

Experimental support for many of the key hypotheses in *Personality and Psychotherapy* came from research that Miller and others performed in the psychology laboratories at Yale. One series of experiments involved teaching animals to be afraid of something they desperately wanted. Hungry rats were first trained to run down a straight wooden alley to a goal box, where they were rewarded with a small amount of food; then the same animals were given a second series of trials, in which they received a painful electric shock as soon as they reached the goal box. Finally they were returned to the starting gate and allowed to move about freely. Almost all the animals subjected to these contradictory lessons showed evidence of what Miller called approach-avoidance conflict. They would start running, go part way toward the goal, stop, back up a bit, go forward a few more steps, stop again, and continue to vacillate in a pattern that Miller described as "increasingly slower approaches and sudden withdrawals." This behavior was almost a parody in physical terms of the agonizing indecision characteristic of many neurotics, who, in the authors' words, "seem to be unable to go forward far enough to reach their goals or away far enough to forget them." The creation of aberrant behavior in white rats was nothing new; Pavlov himself had induced experimental neuroses in laboratory animals by manipulating stimuli under conditions that apparently put an unbearable strain on the subjects' ability to adapt. But Miller believed that a detailed analysis of approach-avoidance conflict in terms of learning theory would lead to a better understanding of the principles that govern both normal and aberrant behavior in human beings.

To laymen, reports of behavioral research often have a faintly ludicrous ring. When behaviorists are not busy comparing rats to men, they seem to be laboring to bring forth mice—that is, seeking elaborate answers to intentionally naïve questions. And yet the strategy of rethinking a problem from the ground up often pays dividends when the questions begin to get more complicated. For Miller, the underlying question has always been: What motivates behavior? Why do organisms respond to stimuli in the first place? Or, to put it entirely in laymen's terms, why does anyone do anything? Miller's basic assumption in the approach-avoidance experiments was that every move a rat made in the alley was the product of opposing motivational forces: a hunger drive and a fear drive. *How* an organism responds to a specific drive stimulus is determined partly by innate, physiological factors and partly by previous learning experiences. A lizard, being cold-blooded, may seek a sunny rock when the temperature drops suddenly; a field mouse will be more likely to head for its burrow; a man may shut a window or put on a sweater or throw another log on the fire or pound on his radiator, depending on which response has been most consistently rewarded in similar situations in the past.

Of course, organisms are often under the lash of more than one drive. In the normal course of events, a conflict between two incompatible drives will be resolved in favor of the drive that happens to be stronger at the moment. (This might be called the "eat-first-talk-later principle.") But according to Miller's careful analysis, the rats suffering from approach-avoidance conflict in the alley are trapped on a kind of motivational seesaw where every response prompted by one drive tends to tip the balance in favor of the other drive, thus making progress in either direction impossible to sustain. The sequence leading up to this uneasy equilibrium presumably goes something like this: After his initial, contradictory lessons, the rat is returned to the starting gate at the safe end of the alley. There he feels more hungry than afraid, so he starts to run toward the distant goal. Since the hunger drive is based primarily on innate physiological factors, the motivation to get food should not vary significantly in strength from one end of the alley to the other. But fear is primarily a learned drive; that is, although we are born with the physiological equipment that goes into the fear response, we generally must learn what to be afraid of. Each painful experience we survive teaches us to respond to certain cues in the environment as warning signals, and the more reminiscent these cues are of the original source of pain the greater the fear they evoke. Thus, the fear becomes stronger as the rat moves nearer to the place where he was shocked originally. Theoretically, as the rat moves down the alley toward the feared and desired goal there will be some point at which the drives of hunger and fear are in perfect equilibrium. But if the rat's forward momentum carries him past this point, fear will suddenly replace hunger as the dominant drive, causing a drastic change in the rat's behavior. The animal will stop, reverse direction, and begin moving away from the goal—until he overshoots the equilibrium point in reverse, whereupon he will turn around and dart forward once more, motivated by hunger, only to be yanked back on the same invisible leash when his fear drive again becomes stronger than his hunger drive. And since the relative strength of the two drives will also fluctuate some-what with the passage of time, the rat will be forced to shuttle back and forth within a narrow range indefinitely—until something happens to shatter the impasse and establish new behavioral priorities.

The authors of *Personality and Psychotherapy* go on to interpret many examples of neurotic behavior in human beings as symptoms of approach-avoidance conflict—usually with sex instead of hunger as the physiological drive that prompts approach, and with the dimensions of approach and avoidance measured not in spatial terms but in socially and culturally defined sequences of events. For example, in the case of an unhappy bachelor who is painfully shy with girls, Miller and Dollard suggest that the graded sequence of "attending a mixed social event, being introduced to a person of the opposite sex, making a telephone call, having a casual date, having a more serious date, engagement, wedding ceremony" may be analogous to the progression of warning signals impinging on the rat as he moves down the alley toward the goal he has learned to desire and fear. This kind of behavioral analysis points up the futility of trying to push a neurotic toward his stated goal by encouragement or exhortation—tactics usually resorted to by well-meaning relatives and friends. At any moment, the neurotic is probably as close to his goal as his conflicting desires and inhibitions will allow, and since neither drive can be satisfactorily reduced in the normal manner, he remains in a state of constant tension. Miller's conflict theory also helps to clarify the therapeutic strategy of psychoanalysis. The best way out of an approach-avoidance impasse is not to strengthen the patient's approach drive but to reduce the fear drive—to weaken resistance, as the Freudians would say—so that the patient can proceed toward his goal without encountering an unbearable level of anxiety. By verbal means, the psychoanalyst can help the patient unlearn the responses that are detrimental to his long-range interests. But the neurotic cannot be cured until he tries out new responses in the real world and finds his behavior rewarded rather than greeted with the punishment that his earlier learning experiences (going all the way back to childhood) have led him to expect.

Personality and Psychotherapy is generally conceded—even by those who do not share its assumptions or conclusions—to be a model of scientific exposition, and it is still widely used as a textbook in undergraduate psychology courses. In a sense, the book makes an excellent introduction to learning theory, because most people have no trouble accepting a strict stimulus-response account of the compulsive, obviously driven behavior of the unhappy neurotic. The behaviorists' assertion that *everything* we do obeys the same stimulus-response principles is much harder to accept, and harder still to demonstrate in a laboratory.

Both Pavlov and Thorndike assumed that their rigorously controlled experiments with a carefully limited range of variables had laid bare certain laws of behavior common to all higher organisms. Their experimental procedures and the theories they formulated to explain their data turned out to be extremely useful to succeeding generations of behavioral scientists. Yet Pavlov's and Thorndike's insights into behavior did not completely coincide, and this meant that the exact relationship between classical conditioning and instrumental learning remained a mystery. Did the two processes of behavioral adaptation represent two distinct stages of evolutionary development? Was one a special case of the other? Or were they merely two different manifestations of a still more basic learning process, whose underlying principles had yet to be discovered? Hull's group at the Institute of Human Relations sought the answers to these questions in a thorough analysis of the mechanism of reinforcement.

Even casual observation reveals that the same events that make good unconditioned stimuli in Pavlovian experiments—such as the delivery of food and the administration of electric shock—make either good rewards or good drive stimuli for trial-and-error learning. And in either situation a delay of as little as twenty seconds in the arrival of a reward or a punishment can be fatal to the reinforcing effect. In trying to account for these and similarly suggestive parallels, Hull advanced the hypothesis that there was at bottom only one kind of learning, achieved through only one kind of reinforcement mechanism, which he identified as drive reduction. Hull's *Principles of Behavior* was published in 1943, and it has served as a touchstone for learning theorists ever since. The proponents of alternative hypotheses—and there have been many—have usually found it necessary to come to terms with drive reduction in one way or another. Among the leading behaviorists, only Skinner and his followers profess to ignore the issue entirely; Skinner maintains that a behaviorist has enough to do studying the effect of different schedules of reinforcement on response rates, without worrying about why rewards work in the first place.

This puzzle is precisely what Miller has spent most of his career worrying about. In fact, he confesses that his unceasing efforts to explain why rewards work have laid him open to the charge of being "emotionally fixated" on the drive-reduction hypothesis. But his behavior is easy to explain in terms of his own theories. If Miller has been loyal to the drive-reduction hypothesis, it is only because he has found the theory both stimulating and rewarding. To a scientist —a man with a passion for parsimony in the explanation of natural phenomena—it is certainly tempting, as Miller puts it, to try to account for all reinforcement by a single physiological mechanism. And the concept of drive reduction does lend itself to experimental manipulation: Find the source of strong stimulation and you can control behavior. But, as most laboratory animals soon learn, the path to a reward is not necessarily smooth or straight. While Miller's efforts to validate the drive-reduction hypothesis have been inconclusive in themselves, the behavioral insights that he gained, the physiological knowledge that he acquired, and the experimental techniques that he perfected all turned out to be indispensable to his later attack on the problem of visceral learning.

From the beginning, it was clear that drive reduction constituted a satisfactory account of what happens when a rat learns to escape from a strong external stimulus like electric shock. The electric shock drives the rat into a frenzy of activity, and the sudden reduction in stimulation at the moment of escape reinforces the immediately preceding response. (It can even be shown that the larger the reduction in voltage the more effective the learning.) The trouble comes with behavior motivated by the so-called appetitive drives, such as hunger, thirst, and sex. Although everyone is familiar with the discomforts of hunger pangs, parched throat, and sexual frustration, even Miller concedes that the strong form of the drive-reduction hypothesis runs counter to our "instinctive judgment," which tells us that it is usually "pleasant stimulation, rather than relief from pain, that one seeks in food and drink, and especially in sex." The question is: Can this instinctive judgment about the appetites be totally mistaken? What kind of internal event actually prompts us to seek food—before the act of eating gets all mixed up with social imperatives? As Miller points out, most people in our affluent society, including most experimental psychologists, have never themselves experienced the sensation of extreme hunger. But experiments with laboratory animals indicate that the satisfaction of hunger has exactly the same effect on the learning process as an escape from electric shock. A hungry rat will learn to perform virtually any response that is rewarded by food, but once he has enough to eat, food ceases to function as a reward. We say that the animal is satiated. In the same way, a rat subjected to electric shock can be rewarded with successive reductions in voltage—but once the voltage is reduced to zero, no more learning on the basis of that particular drive can occur. The two kinds of reinforcing events definitely have more in common than meets the eye. In Miller's words, "There seems to be a close relationship between the operations that produce reinforcement and those that produce satiation." And yet the burden of proof clearly falls on those who argue, as Miller did, that satiation is produced not by getting too much of a good thing but by the total elimination of an unpleasant drive stimulus. In an effort to prove his case, Miller began to turn his attention to what went on during the learning process *inside* the organism, where the glandular and visceral factors that affect the strength of the appetitive drives could be studied more directly.

The drive-reduction hypothesis implies that the reinforcing effect of food can be independent of any pleasant taste or texture. Once we are weaned from the breast, we must learn to eat some things and to avoid others. Any organism that cannot learn to like things that are good for it will probably not survive. But if the primary reinforcement for successful food-seeking behavior is not a pleasant tingle on the tongue, what is it? How does an organism learn that it has stumbled across a nutritious substance (and, conversely, how does it learn not to stuff itself with substances that offer no real nourishment)? The basic challenge for the drive-reduction hypothesis was to show how such learning could take place despite the long delay between the act of eating and the restoration of depleted tissues throughout the body. In a classic experiment that was first published in 1952, Miller and a research associate inserted plastic tubes in the stomachs of white rats so that the animals could be fed without being able to taste the food. The rats were then placed in a simple T-maze which had two distinctively decorated arms. Whenever a rat entered one of these arms, he was rewarded with an injection of enriched milk. Whenever he entered the other, an equal amount of non-nutritive fluid was injected into his stomach. If food functioned as a reward solely because of its taste, no learning should have taken place in the maze. Yet after a number of trials on both sides of the T, the animals consistently chose the milk side. In other words, they had learned to locate the nourishment on the basis of sensations in the digestive tract alone—a finding that fitted in perfectly with a drive-reduction explanation of reinforcement. (There is apparently a hunger center in the brain that is aroused by food deprivation, and this center sets off the unpleasant sensations usually associated with extreme hunger. Miller and other researchers have shown that the act of eating immediately quiets these unpleasant sensations, although exactly how the arousal and quieting of this center is connected to tissue needs is not yet fully understood.)

Other experiments, however, raised some difficult questions about the drive-reduction hypothesis. For instance, food taken by mouth turned out to be an even stronger reward for rats than food injected into the stomach. To square this result with drive reduction, Miller had to show that a mouthful of food also produced a greater reduction in hunger than the same amount of food injected into the stomach. One way to measure the relative strength of the hunger drive in two groups of animals is to see how much each group eats when food is made freely available. Miller and his associates allowed one group of rats to swallow exactly fourteen cubic centimeters of milk from a dish; another group was given the same amount of milk by stomach injection. Then both groups were allowed to drink as much milk as they wanted. The animals who had been allowed to drink their nourishment in the first part of the experiment were markedly less hungry than the animals who had received injections of milk. This proved that there was an important mouth component to the hunger drive as well as a stomach component. But what was the relation between the two? If food in the mouth always produced a prompt reduction in hunger, why did people sometimes talk about whetting the appetite with a pre-dinner snack? Why did some animals appear hungrier *after* eating a small pellet of lab chow? For that matter, how could the drive-reduction hypothesis explain the familiar experience of the cocktail drinker who is unaware of a craving for food until he eats his first peanut? Was it possible that the drive stimulation decreased momentarily with the first nibble of food and then rebounded to an even higher level as soon as the mouth was empty—only to start dropping again when a sufficient amount of food reached the stomach? In order to answer questions like these, Miller had to have some way of monitoring the reactions of all the affected organs and glands while a subject chewed, swallowed, and digested food. This meant that if he was serious about putting the drive-reduction hypothesis to a conclusive test, he would have to delve even deeper into the physiology of the learning organism.

There was good reason to believe that the neural activity set off throughout the body by food deprivation was coordinated in some kind of central switchboard, and there was evidence that the functions of this drive center could be studied with the help of a relatively new research tool, known as electrical stimulation of the brain, or ESB. In the 1930s, a Swiss physiologist named Walter Rudolf Hess had perfected a method for mapping specialized brain structures by anchoring very fine electrodes within the brain tissue of freely moving animals. One of Hess's discoveries was that the application of a weak electrical current to certain focal points in the hypothalamus of a cat would cause the subject to exhibit all the overt signs of extreme fear. As Hess described it, the cat looked and acted afraid, even though such stimulation had been shown to be painless and no comparable reaction had ever been elicited from any of the adjacent areas of the cat's brain. The implications were fascinating. Could it be that the hypothalamus, a primitive structure deep in the base of the brain, contained the switchboard for the cat's fear drive? Was this the place where warning signals from the peripheral sense organs were processed, and orders for appropriate motor responses were dispatched to organs and muscles throughout the body? And could a burst of electrical stimulation actually mimic the incoming neural signals and set off a typical fear response?

Miller's interest in the hypothalamus as a possible drive

center had been heightened by research into the neural regulation of hunger, performed in the late 1940s and early 1950s at the Yale School of Medicine. When certain parts of the hypothalamus were destroyed by surgery, experimental animals stopped eating and literally starved to death, even though they were surrounded by food. Destruction of certain other parts of the hypothalamus had the opposite effect: The animals seemed unable to stop eating, and kept nibbling available food until they became enormously fat. In order to find out whether the hypothalamus actually held the key to the life-or-death responses associated with the primary appetites and emotions, Miller and one of his graduate students, Warren W. Roberts, joined forces in the fall of 1953 with José M. R. Delgado, a neurophysiologist at Yale. Using a combination of physiological and behavioral techniques, the researchers were able to show that cats stimulated in the fear areas not only looked frightened but would also perform previously learned escape responses, and would even learn new responses to avoid further stimulation. Miller concluded that a burst of ESB in the right place did have all the functional properties of a drive. The fact that drives could be manipulated electrically suggested that normal ups and downs in drive strength could be monitored with some kind of electrical pickup. And if this was so, then it might be possible to determine the validity of the drive-reduction hypothesis once and for all. Miller and his associates began looking for ways to record moment-to-moment changes in the hunger drive with implanted electrodes. But before they could overcome the technical problems involved, a team of researchers at McGill University—James Olds and Peter Milner—announced that they had discovered a focal point in the hypothalamus where ESB acted not as a drive stimulus but as a *pleasant* reward. That is, once an animal was given a taste of such stimulation, he would learn to press a bar repeatedly to get additional bursts of current in the same target area—an area that came to be known, perhaps inevitably, as the "pleasure center." Subsequent experiments showed that many animals actually preferred this form of self-stimulation to conventional rewards like food and drink.

At first glance, the work of Olds and Milner—which indicated that reinforcement could result from an increase in stimulation—seemed to deal a fatal blow to the strong version of the drive-reduction hypothesis. But the task of probing the brain had just begun, and the interpretation of the pioneering experiments proved to be far more complicated than any of the pioneers had dreamed. As Miller wrote a few years later, "We have learned . . . that in exploring the behavioral effects of electrical stimulation of the brain, it is unsafe to leave untested any possibility, no matter how implausible it seems." On one hand, there appeared to be no limit to the use of electrical stimulation as an instrument of behavioral control: Miller and his students eventually found a point at which ESB elicited eating in rats that had just been fed to satiation; other researchers reported that bursts of ESB could cause normal monkey mothers to desert their newborn babies, and docile house cats to attack their masters; and, in a unique demonstration that revealed Dr. Delgado's flair for the dramatic, a charging bull with a remote-controlled electrode in its brain was halted by a signal from a portable radio transmitter concealed in a red cape being waved by none other than Dr. Delgado. On the other hand, as the evidence accumulated, many experimental psychologists began to suspect that using ESB to investigate complex neural mechanisms was roughly equivalent to aiming a bolt of lightning at a television set in order to map out the circuitry. The weak electric current delivered to the target areas in the brain was actually far in excess of the voltage generated during the normal transmission of nerve impulses. This meant that a single burst of ESB might fire two or ten or even a hundred adjacent neurons simultaneously, so it was difficult, if not impossible, to tell whether the resulting behavior corresponded in any meaningful way to the organism's normal response patterns. For example, Warren Roberts discovered a focal point in the cat's brain where stimulation had a paradoxical effect, first rewarding and then aversive. (A trained animal would press a lever to turn on such stimulation, press another lever to turn it off, and then alternate between the two levers indefinitely.) This was a curious phenomenon, no matter how you looked at it—but its significance depended somewhat on whether a single neural mechanism was involved, or two separate but related mechanisms, or two functionally independent mechanisms that just happened to lie near each other at this point in the brain.

Much of the early ESB work relied on more or less random probing of brain structures to see what interesting effects might turn up. While Miller and his associates attacked the problem as systematically as possible, their discovery that an eating-control center in the rat's lateral hypothalamus could be triggered by electrical stimulation was actually a lucky accident. In the summer of 1955, after having spent more than a year perfecting their techniques, Miller's research team implanted electrodes in approximately one hundred rats and began conducting elaborate tests to see if stimulation at any point would elicit true motivated behavior such as eating, drinking, aggression, fear, or sex. To their great disappointment, they found none. But some of the rats did show the "reward-aversion" behavior that Roberts had seen earlier in cats; and to get some return from all the work they had done, Miller's team began devising new experiments to take advantage of this paradoxical side effect.

During one of these experiments, a researcher named Ted Coons noticed that a reward-aversion rat who had already been fed to satiation began to nibble at some feces in the test cage when the stimulation was turned on. The time was exactly 11:30 on the night of June 28, 1957. "With admirable ability to capitalize on an unexpected observation," Miller later wrote, "[Coons] threw in some pellets of food and found that the stimulation caused the rats to eat them. Then he spent the rest of the night carefully testing the other ten of his rats. By 6:30 A.M. he had found that stimulation would cause three more of them to eat also. He restrained himself enough to wait until 8:00 A.M. before calling me, and I rushed to the lab to see his results. It was a happy day. We had been looking for something like this for almost two years without any success; now it turned up as a chance observation."

Other experiments established that electrical stimulation in the lateral hypothalamus did have many of the motivational properties commonly associated with the "hunger drive." But Miller's original hope that the discovery would lead to a conclusive test of the drive-reduction hypothesis of reinforcement was frustrated by the inherent limitations of the ESB technique.

To get a better idea of what was actually going on in the electrically stimulated focal points in the brain, Miller and his associates turned to an even newer and potentially more sophisticated research tool: chemical stimulation of the brain. By seeding a target area with small amounts of substances that normally occur in the synapses between nerve cells, the researchers were able to show that the neural control of behavior is, in a literal sense, chemically coded. When one of Miller's students, Sebastian P. Grossman, applied tiny crystals of acetylcholine to a certain area of the hypothalamus, a rat that had just eaten and drunk to satiation started drinking again, but when crystals of norepinephrine were applied to precisely the same area, the satiated rat began to eat instead. Even stranger contrasts appeared when a single substance was applied to different targets a few millimeters apart. A researcher in another lab found that a very small amount of male hormone injected into the rat's hypothalamus could elicit typical male sexual responses or typical maternal behavior in animals of either sex, depending on the site of the injection.

The results of these brain probes were so fascinating in themselves and so suggestive of exciting breakthroughs that for a while Miller found it difficult to interest himself or his graduate students in any other work. But gathering experimental data is one thing, and fitting them into a meaningful pattern is another. It was clear that the brain was the last frontier of both physiology and psychology—the ultimate test of man's ability to understand himself. The use of electrical and chemical stimulation had so far provided a few tantalizing glimpses of the brain's operation—just enough to make men realize how crude even their most advanced theoretical models were. The drive-reduction hypothesis was a prime example; some experiments seemed to support it, others to contradict it. The conclusive test that Miller had hoped for would have to wait until more was known about the brain mechanisms themselves—and in the meantime there was a good chance that someone would devise a broader, more useful hypothesis to make sense out of the mass of new material emerging from the laboratories. While keeping an eye on all these developments, in his own lab and elsewhere, Miller was eager to apply what had already been learned to a closely related and long-neglected problem: the instrumental conditioning of visceral responses.

In 1957 Miller came across an English translation of a book by K. M. Bykov, a Russian physiologist who headed a laboratory in Leningrad devoted to behavorial research in the Pavlovian manner. Bykov's book (originally published in the Soviet Union in 1941) gave a detailed account of the creation of conditioned reflexes involving all kinds of internal functions. Miller was especially impressed by evidence that such deeply buried visceral responses as the formation of urine in the kidneys, contractions of the uterus, and the ejection of red blood cells from the spleen could be classically conditioned to a neutral stimulus (just as a dog could be conditioned to salivate at the ringing of a bell). Bykov's success in bringing a wide range of visceral responses under such precise stimulus control prompted Miller to reexamine his own research priorities. Since he was committed to the view that there is a fundamental unity to all learning, he had to assume that whatever Bykov and his co-workers had accomplished using the techniques of classical conditioning could be duplicated by a researcher using the techniques of instrumental learning. In fact, looking back on his early days at the Institute of Human Relations, he found it remarkable that none of Hull's students had made a serious effort to investigate the possibility of visceral learning. "With so many other people insisting that it couldn't be done, even the smallest positive result would have been a terrific coup for our theory," Miller commented recently. As for himself, he could only conclude, "I may have dodged this particular application of Hull's theory because I felt that it might be refuted here, and I was unconsciously reluctant to face this possible outcome— either out of loyalty to Hull or because the theory was so useful in my other work."

Having taken almost twenty-five years to confront this challenge, Miller could understand the reluctance of a new generation of graduate students to join him in the search for a phenomenon that all the standard psychology text-books—and such acknowledged giants in the field as Skinner—agreed did not exist. "The belief that it is impossible for the stupid autonomic nervous system to exhibit the more sophisticated instrumental learning was so strong that for more than a decade it was extremely hard for me to get any psychology students, or even paid assistants, to work seriously on the problem," Miller told a recent conference of behavioral scientists. "I almost always ended up by letting them work on something they did not think was so preposterous." Out of necessity, his earliest investigations of visceral learning, in 1958 and 1960, were conducted with the aid of a Yale undergraduate majoring in psychology and a research assistant with an M.S. in physiology. Using food as a reward, Miller first tried to teach animals to increase their stomach contractions and to slow down their heartbeats. Although the preliminary tests were slightly encouraging in each case, it took so long to design the experiments, set up the apparatus, and train the animals that his student collaborators graduated or left the university for other reasons before conclusive results could be obtained. In 1961 Miller had to abandon what he affectionately called a "harebrained" scheme to teach rabbits to control the flow of blood through their ears, because his collaborator decided to shift to a more conventional project for a Ph.D. dissertation. Finally, in 1964, Miller persuaded a graduate student, Alfredo Carmona, to carry through an experiment in which thirsty dogs were rewarded with a drink of water whenever their spontaneous bursts of salivation increased or decreased from an empirically established baseline. As the training proceeded, the dogs that were consistently rewarded for increases began to salivate more, and the dogs that were consistently rewarded for decreases began to salivate less. It certainly looked as if the dogs had learned to work for their rewards

—even though this work involved the regulation of a glandular reflex that was supposed to be beyond the organism's voluntary control.

But the results of one experiment were hardly sufficient to overturn what Miller called "the strong traditional belief" within the scientific community that visceral and glandular responses could not be modified by instrumental conditioning. Besides, the results were somewhat ambiguous. As Miller himself noted, one could not rule out the possibility that the dogs had "cheated" by learning to perform some unobserved skeletal response—chewing or panting, say—that indirectly affected the rate of salivation. (Similar objections had been raised a few years earlier when researchers at other laboratories claimed success in instrumentally conditioning the heart rate of human subjects.) Theoretically there˙was only one way to be sure that a specific change in an internal function was the product of genuine visceral learning, and that was to immobilize every skeletal muscle in the subject's body without interfering with the neural control of the visceral organs and glands. Unlikely as it may sound, there was a drug available that fitted this bill precisely. The drug was *d*-tubocurarine—a refined form of the deadly nerve poison curare, which is decocted by South American Indians from the roots, stems, and bark of jungle plants. Medical researchers had discovered that curare works by paralyzing the end plates of the motor nerves linked to the skeletal muscles, including those muscles involved in breathing. Victims of curare-dipped darts generally die within minutes from respiratory failure. But the sensory nerves and the muscles of the internal organs (including the heart and the circulatory system) are apparently not affected. This means that animals—or people—paralyzed by curare can be kept alive indefinitely with a mechanical respirator, and although they are literally unable to move a muscle, they remain fully aware of all external and internal stimuli. (Before the unique selectivity of curare was understood, the drug was used experimentally in the 1940s as a surgical anesthetic. Since the patients were completely immobilized, it was assumed that they felt nothing during the operation. When the effects of the drug wore off and the patients started screaming that they had suffered through every cut of the knife, observers tended to dismiss their accounts as hallucinatory—until a surgeon voluntarily curarized himself and discovered that curare did not prevent pain but only kept the victims from expressing their agony.)

Another of Miller's graduate students, Jay Trowill, decided to see if he could teach curarized animals to modify the rate of their heartbeats for a reward. Since there are not many ways to reward a paralyzed animal, Trowill and Miller settled on electrical stimulation of the previously established "pleasure centers" of the rat's hypothalamus. Trowill spent three years perfecting the techniques for this experiment, while Miller worried that he had sent his young associate up a blind alley. No one knew whether a curarized rat could learn to do anything, much less gain control of its most vital internal function. But when the experiment was completed, in 1966, Trowill had managed to train one group of rats to speed up their hearts and a second group to slow down their hearts. Although the changes in heart rate were only 5 per cent in each direction, Miller felt sufficiently encouraged by the results to embark on an ambitious series of experiments designed to anticipate and overcome all the conceivable objections of the skeptics who still maintained that visceral learning was impossible. During the next few years Miller, a postdoctoral student named Leo DiCara, and a succession of collaborators demonstrated that learned control of the heart rate could be shaped to produce significantly greater changes (one animal slowed its heart from 530 beats a minute to 230), that such control could be made contingent upon a distinctive pattern of cues (some rats learned to slow their hearts more readily when a light-and-tone signal was switched on during the training sessions), and that this learning could be retained, without further instruction, for at least three months. To show how specific such training could become, Miller and DiCara taught some rats to blush in one ear at a time. To show that visceral learning was not limited to cardiovascular responses, Miller and his associates taught rats to modify other bodily functions—ranging from intestinal contractions to the rate of urine formation in the kidney. And, to show that visceral learning did not depend on the peculiar properties of ESB as a reinforcement, changes in heart rate were secured using the standard reward of escape from a painful stimulus. In the course of these experiments, Miller shifted his base of operations from Yale to Rockefeller University, where his continuing research into visceral learning attracted worldwide attention within the scientific community.

Although the techniques and tools developed in Miller's laboratory for the visceral-learning project were far more sophisticated than anything he had used in earlier experiments, it was his long detour into the physiological aspects of drive that had provided much of the technical know-how required for the subsequent work. For a simple training session in heart control, the subject—a healthy, "experimentally naïve" white rat—had to be prepared several days in advance by a lab technician. First, the animal was anesthetized and the top of its skull was laid bare with surgical instruments. Then the technician bored two precisely positioned holes in the skull bone with a jeweler's tiny drill, and two small enamel-sheathed electrodes were inserted through these holes until the exposed metal tips (actually the points of steel sewing needles) came to rest in one of the "pleasure centers" of the brain. A bright green plastic socket that looked a little like a hi-fi jack was permanently anchored to the skull bone with jewelers' screws and a blob of acrylic cement such as dentists use.

After a few days of convalescence in its home cage, the rat was brought back to the lab and given an injection of *d*-tubocurarine, which rendered it completely limp in a few seconds. Working very quickly, the technician pulled a respirator mask (fashioned from the end of a toy balloon) over the animal's nose and jaw; a moment later air was being pumped in and out of its lungs—through two flexible plastic tubes connected to the respirator mask—in a rhythm closely approximating the normal breathing cycle. Outside leads were then plugged into the skull socket; another electrode was attached to a shaved patch of skin on the rat's chest; and the animal was placed on an electrically warmed pallet inside a laboratory isolation chamber—a metal box that resembled a shallow wall oven.

The isolation chamber was connected by a tangle of color-coded wires to other pieces of equipment in the room —an oscilloscope, a programing console, a polygraph. The electrode on the rat's chest picked up signals generated by the beating heart and fed them into one channel of the polygraph, where they were converted into the up-and-down movements of a pen pressing against a continuously unwinding roll of graph paper. A rat's heart normally beats about four hundred and twenty times a minute, but the interval between beats is never absolutely regular. Each heartbeat of the curarized rat was represented by a spike traced on the graph paper. If the rat was being taught to decrease its heart rate, an electronic trigger automatically delivered a burst of rewarding brain stimulation whenever the pause between spikes was long enough to meet a predetermined criterion. A second channel on the polygraph recorded the beginning and the end of each reward period, and so the polygraph provided a permanent log of the learning process.

Once a teaching machine like this has been set up, the researcher theoretically has nothing to do until the lesson is over. But researchers, who are fond of citing the general law "Anything that can go wrong will go wrong," know that the equipment requires constant watching, especially in the early stages of an experiment. At any moment, there may be a short circuit in the electronic trigger, or the artificial respirator may come out of phase, or the oscilloscope may start acting up, or the pens of the polygraph may become wedged against each other. Even when the equipment is operating smoothly, the temptation is all but irresistible to gather around the polygraph and kibitz, cheering the rat on when the ink tracings show that he is making steady progress in his lesson, or groaning in despair when he seems unable to figure out what is being asked of him.

Teaching people to modify visceral responses is much easier in some ways—and much harder in other ways—than training rats. On one hand, nothing could be easier than rewarding the response of a fully conscious human subject who is eager to cooperate; a word of encouragement, or even an impersonal signal that stands for such a word, will do. The problem is knowing when *not* to reinforce. The instructor must be careful to withhold rewards whenever his highly motivated subjects try to mimic the desired visceral adjustment by doing things with their skeletal muscles. Miller and Dworkin refer to any attempt to attain a reward by nonvisceral means as "cheating." For instance, when hypertensive patients are asked to lower their blood pressure, they invariably begin by altering their breathing. It happens that a sudden deep breath will produce a temporary drop in blood pressure. This decrease cannot be maintained and therefore has no medical significance, but the patient will keep repeating the respiratory maneuver as long as the machine keeps rewarding it. Obviously, no real therapeutic progress can be made unless this competing response is recognized for what it is and extinguished by lack of reinforcement. The subject is not consciously trying to cheat; the organism as a whole simply follows the path of least resistance to a reward. But since there is no way— short of curarization—to guarantee that all potential avenues of skeletal cheating have been closed, each visceral-training session takes on the nature of a game. The instructor's basic strategy is to make cheating so difficult—by building checks and double checks into the monitoring system—that the subject can earn the reward only by modifying the internal mechanism itself. According to learning theory, this strategy should be effective for any visceral or glandular response under neural control; the only practical limit is the ingenuity of the researcher in finding ways to measure and reward spontaneous changes as soon as they occur.

There may, of course, be some skeletal maneuvers that have a significant effect on the patient's health, and some biofeedback researchers ignore the problem of cheating entirely—they are more concerned with getting therapeutic results than with worrying about how the patient achieves them. Miller's primary interest, however, has never been simply to extend man's control over his bodily functions. Despite the potential medical applications, his goal in this research, as in all his other work, was to gain a better insight into the fundamental laws that govern human behavior. Once he was convinced that visceral learning was possible with the right kind of feedback, the next logical step was to ask what role this ability plays in the ordinary life history of the organism, since, as he put it, one would hardly expect the forces of evolution to create a mechanism that had "no normal function other than that of providing my students with subject matter for publications."

It is easy to see how the shaping of skeletal behavior through reward and punishment improves the individual's chances of getting food, avoiding pain, and reproducing his species in hostile surroundings. The survival value of purely visceral learning is not so apparent. In order to survive, all warm-blooded animals must maintain a fairly constant internal environment. The homeostatic balance for each species, however, seems to be wired into the individual's nervous system at birth. Barring major organic damage, a man's temperature tends to remain at about 98.6 degrees Fahrenheit; his blood pressure usually hovers around 120/70; his heart normally beats something like seventy times a minute. And when physical strain or illness causes a drastic deviation from these norms, the organism automatically does what is necessary to compensate. This, at least, is the traditional view of homeostasis. One famous physiologist of the early twentieth century referred to the self-corrective tendencies of the reflexes mediated by the autonomic nervous system as "the wisdom of the body." The clear implication was that the less interference from the higher mental processes the better. But the recent up-surge of interest in biofeedback training has forced behavioral scientists to take a new look at the relationship between the so-called higher and lower levels of the nervous system.

There is no real contradiction between reflex behavior and instrumental learning. Learning builds on innate reflexes. Before a man can learn to swing a golf club properly, he must be able to keep his balance and to make all the separate skeletal adjustments that go into a golf swing, and to "read" the kinesthetic feedback from the muscles being used. What a man actually learns from reinforced practice, Miller says, is "to combine innate behavioral units at a given time, under the control of a specific stimulus, with the appropriate force, and in the appropriate direction." It may be that the innate homeostatic reflexes set only the broad limits for each visceral function, and that evolution has provided a capacity for instrumental learning that can be used for what might be called fine tuning in early infancy. It is also possible that this capacity is available as an emergency backup system for the preservation of homeostasis in the mature organism. There is no longer any doubt that the internal environment can be modified through the medium of classical conditioning. For instance, one of Bykov's colleagues carefully documented the effect of habitual behavior on the normal metabolic rate—the rate at which body cells use oxygen. Two laborers in a tire factory were asked to stand aside and watch their comrades go through a typical work day. The work called for brief periods of great physical exertion followed by slightly longer rest periods. Tests made on the two idle men showed that their oxygen consumption rose and fell during the day in a pattern that closely paralleled the normal alternation of work and rest periods. Apparently their daily routine had conditioned them to respond in a certain way to specific stimuli—the factory whistle, the sound of the foreman's voice, the sight of their fellow workers. When these stimuli were present, the two laborers went through all the metabolic adjustments associated with physical labor, even though no actual demands were being made on their skeletal muscles.

Miller believes that in the normal course of events some people may unconsciously make even more specific—and more permanent—homeostatic adjustments as a result of instrumental learning. The habits formed in this way will not necessarily be beneficial to the organism in the long run. For example, Barry Dworkin has worked out a scenario showing how a certain combination of innate and environmental factors could lead to a condition like primary hypertension. It can be assumed that, just as some people are

born with superior physical equipment for a particular
sport such as football or basketball, there are people who
are born with an above-average ability to control their cardiovascular reflexes. Whether or not they learn to make use
of this talent depends on their circumstances. It happens
that, through a complicated neural tie-in, a sudden rise in
blood pressure results in a *decrease* in the general alertness
or excitability of the organism. The effect appears to be
similar to that produced by a dose of barbiturates used in
the treatment of mild anxiety. According to Dworkin's hypothesis, certain individuals may discover early in life that
they can virtually turn off a disturbing stimulus by raising
their blood pressure. The disturbing stimulus may be external in origin (like a persistent loud noise) or largely
self-inflicted (like the unresolvable tensions of approach-
avoidance conflict). In either case, the immediate effect of
a rise in blood pressure is to prevent the full force of the
disturbance from reaching the cerebral cortex, just as
stuffing cotton in one's ears helps to block out the sound
of a jackhammer. Since even a brief and partial reduction
in a strong stimulus acts as a reward, a person with a talent
for cardiovascular control may develop the habit of calming
himself by raising his pressure whenever he faces an unpleasant situation, just as a person with a different physiological make-up may become addicted to barbiturates. The
implications of this hypothesis, which Miller and Dworkin
hope to test someday, go far beyond the immediate clinical
uses. "If we succeed in proving that instrumental learning
can play a role in the maintenance of homeostasis, we will
have established a principle of major biological importance," Dworkin says.

There is very strong evidence that the requisite feedback
mechanisms exist. Other researchers have shown that impulses from a vast number of internal sensory nerves—
known as "interoceptors"—are constantly ascending from

the viscera to the higher levels of the nervous system, and that the higher levels are constantly acting on such information through a variety of motor channels. But this constant visceral feedback rarely penetrates to the level of subjective awareness, and this is perhaps why Western scientists have found it so hard to accept the existence of a sophisticated communications network serving the internal organs and glands.

For some reason, scientists in Russia and Eastern Europe have taken a more empirical approach to the study of the autonomic nervous system. As early as 1866, I. M. Sechenov, the father of Russian physiology, noted the existence of "dark sensations" originating in the visceral organs and apparently reaching the cerebral cortex. Sechenov was a major influence on Pavlov, who was convinced by his own work on conditioned reflexes that there must be "special analyzers" in the cortex which had the task of "continuously recording the enormous complex of events that happen within the organism." Bykov and his co-workers confirmed this insight for a wide range of visceral responses, and more recently a Hungarian physiologist named György Ádám has conducted detailed studies of the central-nervous-system mechanisms that process information from the viscera. Among other things, his work has shown that some visceral interoceptors are at least as responsive to changing conditions as the five external senses are. For instance, a dog can be trained to discriminate between sensations in its lower intestines which are no more than a few centimeters apart. Ádám has also worked out a method for teaching people to become conscious of sensations in their viscera that are far below the normal threshold of subjective awareness. Miller hopes to make use of Ádám's research on interoception in his own attempts to teach people to control their internal functions. Yet Ádám himself takes a surprisingly conservative view of the practical applications of his work. He sees his experiments as furthering our understanding of the neural mechanisms involved, but he is wary about trying to extend our conscious and voluntary control too far. "The basic prerequisite of the normal functioning of the organism seems to be that interoceptive impulses should remain unconscious," Ádám wrote in a book called *Interoception and Behavior* published in Budapest in 1967. "It can be assumed that the reinforcement of interoceptive . . . impulses other than [those conditioned in early childhood] would constitute too great a stress for higher nervous centers; in other words, to bring into consciousness such internal processes would be pathological." What is even more surprising is that Ádám, who is a painstaking researcher, offers no evidence to support this assumption. Miller's position is that the difference between skeletal and visceral responses— which really comes down to the difference between the somatic and the autonomic branches of the nervous system —has been greatly exaggerated. He believes that, with the improved feedback provided by medical technology, people may someday learn to become at least as aware of the "dark sensations" from the viscera as most adults are of the vague sensations from the skeletal muscles in the torso: "Doctor, I have this slight ache—no, more like a faint throbbing—just below my left shoulder blade and over a bit, and sometimes it feels a little hot, or sort of prickly."

3

Adventures in Self-Control

Yoga, Zen, and the Power of Meditation

Most Westerners are familiar with tales of Indian yogis and other Eastern mystics who achieve unusual bodily control through occult religious practices. Reliable observers have offered numerous eyewitness accounts of such yogic feats as stopping the heart for a minute or two, being buried alive for days or weeks with no ill effects, and walking barefoot over a bed of hot coals. But even in cases where outright fraud seems unlikely, the conventional Western attitude toward these tales has been one of bemused skepticism. In particular, Western scientists have tended to dismiss hearsay evidence concerning the voluntary control of autonomic functions, on the presumption that some kind of skeletal cheating—either conscious or unconscious—was always involved. No one doubted that the practitioners of yoga were brilliant showmen and exquisitely trained physical specimens, but this did not mean that they had anything of real importance to teach Western science.

In the late 1950s, however, a team of Indian and American scientists made an effort to find out exactly what the most proficient yogis could do. The researchers were interested not only in the rumored ability of certain yogis to regulate specific "involuntary" functions at will, but also in the general physiological changes that are supposed to take place during meditation. In 1957 two physiologists, Marion A. Wenger of UCLA and Basu K. Bagchi of the University of Michigan Medical School, traveled four thousand miles across the Indian subcontinent, lugging a portable eight-channel recording machine that operated on flashlight batteries. With this device and appropriate accessories, they were able to record the electrical activity of the brain (EEG), the heart (EKG), and the skeletal muscles (EMG), as well as the electrical resistance of the skin, skin temperature, blood pressure, respiration, and other physiological variables during different yogic exercises.

Locating suitable subjects for the study was not easy. Meditative yogis (sometimes called Raja yogis) are usually deeply religious men; most of those approached by Wenger and Bagchi refused to participate in experiments with electrodes and other instruments attached to their bodies, since they found such trappings incompatible with the spiritual purpose of meditation. Practitioners of the more mundane Hatha yoga—which stresses postural and breathing control as a means of disciplining and purifying the body—were more cooperative. Altogether, Wenger and Bagchi spent five months on the project; they set up their instruments and made recordings in eight different locations, ranging from laboratories and private homes in Calcutta and New Delhi to a secluded cave in the Himalayas. In the end, useful data was obtained from forty-five subjects, including two women.

Three of the subjects were Hatha yogis who claimed that they could "stop the heart." On close examination, it turned out that all three subjects performed the same set of respiratory and skeletal-muscle maneuvers: each took a deep breath and held it, closed his windpipe, locked his chin against his chest, and contracted his chest and abdominal muscles. These maneuvers increased the pressure within the chest cavity. When the pressure became great enough, the veins bringing blood back to the heart were virtually squeezed shut. With little or no blood to pump, the characteristic heart sounds—*lubb-dup, lubb-dup*—could not be heard even with a stethoscope, and no pulse could be felt at the wrist or elsewhere. Given this impressive "evidence," it is easy to see how lay observers, physicians, and the subjects themselves could believe that the heart had stopped. But, according to Wenger and Bagchi, the action of the heart had simply become inaudible as it had no blood to pump. EKG recordings revealed that the heart muscle went right on contracting and expanding at a rapid rate. However, a fourth subject, who claimed not to stop the heart but merely to slow it down, did manage to reduce his heart rate briefly from 63 beats per minute to 24 beats per minute. While his performance too was accompanied by respiratory and skeletal maneuvers, the researchers concluded that no single maneuver or combination of maneuvers could possibly have accounted for such a drastic change.

Another subject gave incontrovertible proof of direct voluntary control over quite a different autonomic function: sweating. A few minutes after receiving a direct command, he could produce drops of perspiration on his forehead without any detectable skeletal-muscle maneuver. (Although he was not aware of it, his systolic blood pressure went up sharply at the same time.) In explaining how he had learned to perspire voluntarily, the subject said that he had spent parts of two winters practicing yoga in a Himalayan cave, wearing nothing but animal skins. Not surprisingly, the extreme cold bothered him; to combat this distraction, his teacher advised him to concentrate on "warmth" and to visualize himself in a hot-weather situation. After six months of practice, he reported gradual success with this method. Later, when he tried the same thing in a more moderate climate, he found that his mental images produced not only sensations of increased warmth but perspiration as well.

By following up numerous leads supplied by friends and colleagues and by using all their persuasive powers, the researchers eventually secured the cooperation of fourteen Raja yogis. The most significant finding to emerge from this part of the study concerned changes in the electrical resistance of the skin during meditation. The resistance of the skin to an electrical current is generally considered to be an involuntary indicator of the subject's level of anxiety; for this reason it is one of the physiological parameters monitored in the familiar lie-detector test. According to most experts, decreased resistance to an electrical current (which can be found, for example, in a subject with sweaty palms) reflects a high level of anxiety. Conversely, skin resistance is supposed to increase as activity within the autonomic nervous system subsides. By this standard of measurement, the meditating yogis—who sat motionless in a lotus position with eyes closed for up to two and a half hours—were *extremely* relaxed. All showed an increase in skin resistance to electricity; the median rise during meditation was 56 per cent greater than that shown by the same subjects during nonmeditative control periods. At the same time, electroencephalographic recordings revealed no evidence of drowsiness, light sleep, dream sleep, deep dreamless sleep, or coma. The prominent EEG pattern of the meditating yogis was a strong, regular alpha rhythm.

Alpha is one of the "brain-wave" patterns typically recorded from awake subjects when electrodes are painlessly attached to various places on the scalp. The actual signals picked up by the electrodes are in the 10-to-100–microvolt range (a microvolt is one-millionth of a volt). These signals must be greatly amplified before they are strong enough to drive a recording pen across an unwinding roll of graph paper. The wavy or jagged ink tracings represent oscillations in voltage that in turn represent the summated electrical activity of many individual cells in the cerebral cortex. When a subject is awake but mentally relaxed and not attending to external stimuli (usually with his eyes closed), the EEG tracing falls into a slow, well-marked rhythm, with peaks and valleys repeated at regular intervals (about 8 to 12 times per second). According to the most widely accepted theory, this alpha rhythm is the result of large numbers of brain cells firing in unison, each synchronized burst of activity producing an EEG signal of relatively high voltage. When a subject is called upon to process sensory information (especially visual stimuli) or to focus on a specific mental task, the alpha rhythm is abruptly blocked or "desynchronized," and beta activity appears. Beta waves are more rapid (13 to 26 cycles per second) than alpha waves, and less regular, presumably because different groups of cells are now firing at different rates. And, with fewer brain cells firing at any given moment, the signals produced are of relatively low voltage.

In normal subjects prolonged alpha activity is often a prelude to sleep. According to Wenger and Bagchi, however, meditating yogis have mastered the ability to go into a state of deep physiological and mental relaxation *without losing consciousness.* No abnormal blood-pressure readings were found in meditating subjects, but in most cases the rate of respiration slowed down markedly; two subjects dropped from about thirteen breaths per minute to only four, and stayed that way for a quarter of an hour.

Whatever the spiritual and physical benefits of this kind of meditative state, the profound "inwardness" of the yoga experience was vividly demonstrated in one of the experiments, which Dr. Bagchi described as follows:

> An elderly Swami after leading an active life of doing public good retired to the Himalayan mountains (Rishikesh). He was a bearded, orange-robed, non-organizational, well-respected individual. He cooperated with us after we appealed to him on two occasions, though he frankly placed the highest value on inner growth and spirituality rather than on scientific experimentation. In spring we brought the machine to his cave near the flowing Ganges River flanked by four-to-five-thousand-foot-high mountains and nature's silent grandeur. Two experiments were done on two days. During his meditation for about twenty-five minutes in the cave, with no electrical shielding, there was the normal well-regulated waxing-and-waning pattern of waking brain waves [alpha], no drowsiness or sleep waves. The skin resistance steadily rose 70 per cent over control period. The tone of extremities seemed markedly reduced, and to all appearances he went into a state of complete withdrawal, even when EKG and palmar electrodes were being put on during the first experiment. Low-intensity sounds within three to five feet, like the shuffling of feet, were not perceived, according to later subjective report; except for a slight shift of the baseline on two occasions no blocking of the brain waves or decrease of palmar electrical resistance (sign of change toward alertness) was seen during slight nearby noise.

Dr. Bal K. Anand, chairman of the Physiology Department at the All-India Institute of Medical Sciences in New Delhi, collaborated with Wenger and Bagchi in their original study; since 1957, he and his colleagues at the Institute have examined more than four hundred yogis under carefully controlled laboratory conditions. While the great majority of subjects gave no proof of unusual physical abilities, a handful performed internal gymnastics that cannot be explained as a result of skeletal cheating. One subject, who had been practicing yoga for five years, could reduce his heartbeat to half the normal rate for fifteen or twenty seconds by blocking the action of the sinoatrial node—the so-called cardiac pacemaker. This was apparently achieved by increasing the firing rate of the vagus nerve, which has an inhibitory effect on heart rhythm. Anand thinks that most if not all meditating yogis slow their hearts through vagal control, and that the yogi who could turn off his pacemaker at will was simply very proficient at this technique. (Dr. Bagchi speculates that it may even be possible for a person to kill himself this way. There are well-documented cases of yogis who announced a desire to "leave the body" permanently, and who then passed away at a specified time and place during a meditative trance in the presence of their friends and disciples.)

In another experiment conducted at Anand's laboratory in New Delhi, an experienced yogi was sealed inside an airtight metal-and-glass box (6 feet by 4 feet by 4 feet) while his EEG, EKG, respiration, and other physiological variables were monitored through electrical leads. From the data obtained, it appears that the tales of yogis being buried alive for days and even weeks to demonstrate their powers may very well be true. Anand's subject was able to slow down his metabolism until he was functioning at less than half his basal metabolic rate. (Basal metabolic rate is a standard measure of the body's activity in an awake but completely relaxed state. To get some idea of the yogi's achievement, body metabolism in a normal person never falls more than 10 or 12 per cent below the basal metabolic rate, even during the deepest sleep.) The yogi was removed from the sealed box only when the oxygen inside fell to a dangerously low level. In public demonstrations in Indian villages, Hatha yogis are usually placed in a freshly dug pit and then covered with six feet of earth. Since there is evidence that such a "grave" is nowhere near so airtight as it seems, a yogi who knew how to lower his metabolism—and therefore his oxygen consumption—could presumably remain buried for long periods with no ill effects.

While following up the earlier EEG studies of meditating yogis, Anand also confirmed that some yogis can voluntarily shut out the external world without falling asleep. He found that the yogis' alpha activity during eyes-closed meditation could not be blocked by a bright light, loud banging noises, the touch of a hot glass tube, or the vibration of a tuning fork. When the yogis were merely sitting quietly and *not* meditating, these same stimuli produced the expected "startle" reaction—an abrupt desynchronization of the alpha rhythm that usually occurs when a person directs his attention to an external source of disturbance.

A similar study of Japanese practitioners of Zen meditation, published in 1966, reveals fascinating parallels to the Indian research on yoga—and fascinating differences as well. Two Japanese scientists, Akira Kasamatsu and Tomio Hirai, recorded the brain waves of forty-eight Zen masters and disciples of varying ages and experience. Recordings were made before, during, and after periods of meditation that lasted about thirty minutes. In the usual Zen fashion, the meditators' eyes remained *open.* Yet a minute or two after they assumed the correct sitting position, alpha waves began to appear in their EEGs. These alpha waves became stronger and slower as meditation continued. In the most experienced meditators, very slow, high-voltage "theta" waves were sometimes seen toward the end of the half-hour period—an unusual occurrence, especially since the theta rhythm was not accompanied by the usual behavioral or neurological signs of drowsiness. Control subjects who sat quietly with their eyes open for thirty minutes showed the beta pattern, indicating normal wakefulness, almost exclusively. (It is interesting to note that the EEG of hypnotized people is not different from that of normal waking subjects. According to most studies, people in deep hypnotic trances show abundant alpha waves when they are sitting calmly with their eyes shut, and predominant beta activity when their eyes are open and they are performing specific tasks suggested by the hypnotist.)

The Japanese researchers also tested the reaction of Zen meditators to mildly disturbing external stimulation—a series of twenty clicks repeated at regular fifteen-second intervals. The results were surprising and provocative. After each click in the series, the alpha rhythm of the Zen meditators was blocked for a few seconds; then it resumed as if nothing had happened. This was in sharp contrast to the uninterrupted alpha of the Indian yogis, whose EEGs indicated that they were virtually impervious to external stimuli. The Zen meditators' reaction also differed sharply from that of a group of nonmeditating control subjects who were exposed to the clicks after they had been sitting long enough with their eyes closed to develop a well-organized alpha rhythm. In these control subjects, the first click completely blocked the alpha waves, but the second and third click had progressively less effect, and the startle reaction all but disappeared after the fourth click. Clearly, the subjects had come to expect the click so it no longer disturbed them. In psychological jargon, they had become habituated to the sound. Kasamatsu and Hirai emphasized the fact that the Zen meditators did *not* become habituated, no matter how many times the click was repeated. To explain why, the researchers turned to the subjects' own descriptions of the meditative experience:

> The Zen masters reported to us that they had more clearly perceived each stimulus than in their ordinary waking state. In [the meditative] state of mind, one cannot be affected by either external or internal stimulus, nevertheless he is able to respond to it. He perceives the object, responds to it, and yet is never disturbed by it. Each stimulus is accepted as stimulus itself and treated as such. One Zen master described such a

state of mind as that of noticing every person one sees on the street but of not looking back with emotional curiosity.

Of the basis of these introspective reports and the electroencephalographic evidence, Kasamatsu and Hirai concluded that Zen meditation produces "a special psychological state" characterized by "relaxed awakening with steady responsiveness." This sounds very much like the descriptions in traditional religious texts of the level of consciousness achieved by diligent Zen meditators: "Whether going or returning, they remain forever unmoved; taking hold of the not-thought which lies in thoughts, in every act of theirs they hear the voice of the Truth."*

Further evidence that meditation can lead to significant physiological changes comes from two scientists at the Harvard Medical School, Robert K. Wallace and Herbert Benson. Their research was conducted not with Indian yogis or Japanese monks but with thirty-six American volunteers, ranging in age from seventeen to forty-one, who had been trained in a technique known as transcendental meditation. This is a form of yoga, especially adapted for use in the West by the Maharishi Mahesh Yogi, that requires no rigorous physical or mental control, no specific belief or faith, and no major changes in life style. It can be learned in three or four hour-long sessions; essentially, the subject is taught a systematic method of perceiving a "suitable" sound (or thought) without concentrating on any specific sensory qualities or intellectual content. The meditator usually practices twice a day for fifteen or twenty minutes at a time, sitting in a comfortable position with his eyes closed. According to the Maharishi, transcendental meditation involves "turning the attention inwards toward the subtler levels of a thought until the mind transcends the experi-

*Hakuin, 1685–1768 A.D., translated by D. T. Suzuki.

ence of the subtlest state of the thought and arrives at the source of the thought."

The thirty-six subjects in the Wallace-Benson study had all been trained by instructors associated with the Students International Meditation Society, based in Los Angeles. Most of them had been practicing transcendental meditation for two or three years, and they had no difficulty meditating in a laboratory setting, despite the elaborate monitoring devices that had to be attached to their bodies. The results of the study were as follows: Almost as soon as meditation began, the subjects' oxygen consumption fell sharply, electrical skin resistance increased considerably, the heart slowed down a few beats per minute, and the EEG showed a marked intensification of slow alpha activity. In addition, the concentration of a substance called blood lactate declined "precipitously." There is evidence that a high concentration of lactate in the blood is correlated with a high level of anxiety. For example, patients with anxiety neurosis show a rise in blood lactate when placed in stressful situations, and an infusion of lactate can not only bring on a full-fledged anxiety attack in such patients but can also trigger symptoms of anxiety in normal subjects. On the other hand, low blood-lactate levels and feelings of "tranquillity" seem to go together.

All in all, Wallace and Benson found that transcendental meditation produces what they call a "wakeful hypometabolic state," characterized by a general quiescence of the autonomic nervous system. This state is in many ways the opposite of the flight-or-fight syndrome, in which the entire body is mobilized (through increased heart rate, higher oxygen consumption, et cetera) to meet an external threat. While the flight-or-fight syndrome has obvious survival value, it may be harmful to an organism that is aroused too often by the incessant alarms and challenges of modern society. The homeostatic controls of an organism under constant stress may deteriorate, leading to chronic high blood pressure, heart malfunctions, and so on.

Although individual reactions and training techniques vary, meditation seems to be a reliable means of putting both mind and body into a lower gear. Successful meditators claim that the benefits range from improved health to profound insights into the nature of the universe. Not surprisingly, outsiders are most intrigued by the "mind over matter" aspect of the meditative state. But the yogis themselves insist that the self-control they achieve can be seen as completely natural once the true relationship between mind, body, and the universe is understood. Speaking across gulfs of language and history, Neal Miller would agree with them. And a number of researchers have begun to explore the possible use of meditative exercises—with or without feedback—as a treatment for the stress-related diseases that plague civilized man.

In trying to isolate the core of the meditative experience, many scientific investigators, as well as some not-so-scientific enthusiasts, have focused on the changes that occur within the brain itself—in particular, the unusual prevalence of alpha activity in the EEG records of meditating subjects. The acknowledged pioneer of alpha-wave-feedback research is Joe Kamiya, formerly of the University of Chicago and now of the Langley Porter Neuropsychiatric Institute in San Francisco. In 1958, while conducting dream research in Chicago, Kamiya asked himself whether there was any way to establish a clear relationship between what a person's brain was doing (as recorded objectively on an EEG machine) and what his mind was doing (as reported verbally by the subject himself). He decided to work with the alpha rhythm because it was relatively easy to record. His earliest experiments showed that if a person was given the proper feedback he could learn to distinguish between "brain-wave state A" (characterized by lots of alpha) and "brain-wave state B" (no alpha).

The training procedure was simple enough. After being hooked up to an EEG machine in a darkened room, the subject was asked to guess from time to time whether he was in state A or state B; as soon as he responded, he was told whether he had guessed right or not. At first the typical performance was exactly what one would expect from chance alone—that is, half the guesses were right and half were wrong. But after an hour or so most subjects had improved their score to about 60 per cent correct. By the third hour, many were guessing right three times out of four; and some subjects went on to achieve 100-per-cent accuracy.

Kamiya followed up his original discovery with a series of ingenious experiments that proved people could learn to produce or suppress alpha voluntarily; the feedback in this instance was a soft tone that went on as soon as alpha waves appeared in the subject's EEG and went off as soon as alpha activity ceased. Kamiya also taught people to sustain alpha over a prolonged period and to modify both the frequency and the amplitude of the waves. But not everyone could learn to control his brain waves. Through informal conversations and formal questionnaires, Kamiya discovered that the subjects who were especially good at increasing their alpha production had generally had experience in some kind of "meditation"; they also tended to be more introspective than unsuccessful subjects, and they had fewer inhibitions about discussing their dreams, thoughts, and feelings. After moving his laboratory to San Francisco, Kamiya made a special effort to recruit subjects who meditated regularly. As expected, these subjects learned to control their alpha rhythm quite easily. They also reported that the high-alpha state was similar in some ways to what they experienced while performing their meditative exercises.

When pressed for details, most high-alpha producers could only say that the experience was pleasant but hard to put into words. Some talked about a mood of "calm passivity." Others described it as "content-free consciousness." One subject said that he felt as if he were "floating about half an inch above my seat." With reports like these appearing in scientific journals, it is hardly surprising that the popular press began to refer to alpha-wave training as "electronic yoga" or "instant Zen," and to the high-alpha state as a new kind of "drugless high." When some researchers found that artists and musicians were better than average at producing alpha waves, the high-alpha state was also linked to "creativity." Commercial exploitation was inevitable. In the late 1960s scores of new firms sprang up to sell alpha-wave expertise and hardware. At one end of the scale, "portable EEG machines" costing hundreds of dollars appeared on the market; prospective buyers were offered the opportunity to "tune in" on their own brain waves. At the other end of the scale, classified ads in youth-oriented newspapers and magazines promised to pass along the secret of this new form of "mind-control" for only five dollars.

Reputable scientists such as Kamiya have pointed out that most of the alpha-feedback machines available for home use are not reliable enough for training purposes. And while do-it-yourself alpha training can probably do no harm, the value of even a successful learning experience remains in doubt. For one thing, learning to identify and control your brain waves through EEG feedback is not quite so exotic as it sounds. The alpha rhythm can be desynchronized by all sorts of voluntary behavior having to do with vision; directing your eyes toward a specific target will do it, and in many cases so will conjuring up a mental image of something you have seen. The verbal reports of subjects who have been trained to increase alpha in the laboratory confirm that there is more than one way to control brain waves. Some successful subjects are quick to make use of the connection between eye movements and EEG feedback; others say that they switch their alpha on and off by shifting from one subjective state to another—from "relaxation" to "tension and vigilance," for example, or from an attitude of "letting go" to one of "holding on." Still other successful subjects report that they have no idea of what they are doing, except that it seems to work.

The undisputed facts of the matter are: 1) Yogis and Zen monks produce an unusual amount of alpha activity during meditation; 2) meditation has a marked and possibly beneficial effect on body metabolism; 3) with EEG feedback many people can learn to increase their alpha activity; 4) artists and musicians seem to excel at this task. From these facts, however, it does not necessarily follow that learning to increase your alpha will bring you all the physiological benefits of meditation—much less such other bonuses as peace of mind and enhanced creativity. The person who learns to switch on his alpha at will, and to prolong a high-alpha state, may have learned no more than to keep his eyes unfixated and his mind free of visual images—a difficult feat of self-control, perhaps, but hardly an earth-shaking one. Consider the following analogy: A middle-aged man is told by his doctor that he should jog a mile every morning to keep in shape. The man notices that after jogging he sweats heavily. The man just happens to be able to sweat voluntarily (like Dr. Anand's yogi). Instead of jogging, the man decides that he can save time and get the same therapeutic effect by sitting in his chair and sweating for ten minutes.

Alpha-wave training may turn out to be a short cut to bodily control, or it may not. As yet, no one really understands the functional relationship between brain-wave patterns, on one hand, and behavior and personality traits, on the other. There are, of course, some intriguing theories.

Certain brain structures below the cerebral cortex play a major role in the maintainance of homeostasis. Taken together, these structures comprise what Dr. Anand calls the "visceral brain." Consciousness and higher-order learning are usually considered to be functions of the cerebral cortex. Anand believes that during the special alpha state associated with yogic meditation the "conscious brain" is able to influence the "visceral brain" in new ways, the most significant result being a temporary lowering of body metabolism. One theoretical advantage of biofeedback is the greater efficiency it promises to bring to this brain-body interaction. The control that a yogi works years to attain could conceivably be learned in a few weeks or months, and the training could be directed at a specific organ or regulatory system. Clinical experiments designed to test this approach are already under way in major research laboratories and hospitals throughout the country.

Clinical Applications

The first attempts to teach human beings to modify "autonomic" functions with the help of feedback signals came in the early 1960s. The results of these experiments were highly controversial. The functions being monitored —heart rate, blood pressure, skin resistance to electricity— seemed to shift in the desired direction during training. But the changes were quite small—on the order of a few beats per minute or a few millimeters of mercury—and critics argued that such changes could easily have been produced by skeletal and respiratory maneuvers that had no long-term medical significance. To rule out this possibility, the researchers devised more and more rigorous experimental controls, but the critics were not satisfied. In the face of such unremitting skepticism, few scientists cared to test their theories in a genuine clinical situation. When Neal Miller and his co-workers announced that their curarized rats were learning to control a variety of visceral functions, biofeedback research with human subjects suddenly became more respectable, and the possibility that sick people might someday benefit from biofeedback training no longer seemed so preposterous.

One of the most persistent and ingenious researchers in this field is Barnard Engel, a psychologist now affiliated with the Baltimore City Hospitals and the National Institute of Child Health and Human Development. Engel has worked out a method of training subjects to speed up or slow down the heart, and he has applied it to the treatment of cardiac arrhythmias—irregularities in the normal pumping rhythm of the heart which, in severe cases, may lead to sudden death. One common arrhythmia is characterized by premature contractions of the left ventricle, the chamber that forces freshly oxygenated blood into the arterial system. In a normal heart, the left ventricle expands and contracts about once a second. In a premature ventricular contraction (PVC), it closes too soon; this may happen as often as thirty times a minute. Some patients are conscious of the irregularity; they say that it feels as if the heart were "skipping a beat." But most people with PVCs do not feel anything unusual, even after their condition has been diagnosed by a physician.

In 1970 Engel and a colleague, Dr. Theodore Weiss, attempted to teach eight patients with PVCs to stabilize their heart rhythm. The training process was long and demanding. Each patient received about fifty training sessions, with as many as three sessions scheduled per day. The average session lasted eighty minutes. During this time the patient lay on a hospital bed in a quiet room with standard EKG electrodes taped to his chest. The signals generated by his beating heart were transmitted to an electrocardiograph connected to a feedback display panel with three colored lights—green, red, and yellow. The green and red lights served as cues for the patient: when the green light came on, he was supposed to make his heart beat faster; when the red light came on, he was supposed to slow his heart down. The yellow light was the "rein-forcer" or reward light; it came on whenever the patient was responding correctly to the other cues. Through this feedback system, the patient could be kept informed about changes in his heart rate on a beat-by-beat basis. Once he had demonstrated the ability to speed up or slow down his heart on cue, he was given the new task of maintaining his heart rate within a predetermined range. As long as he succeeded, the yellow light remained on, signifying a job well done. If the number of beats per minute fell on either side of the acceptable range, the yellow light went off and the appropriate cue light came on. During this stage of training the display panel was programed to flash a special signal—a red light followed immediately by a green light—whenever a PVC occurred. By tagging each premature con-traction in this manner, Engel and Weiss hoped to draw the patient's attention to the faint but distinctive sensations that accompany an abnormal beat. In the final stage of training, the patient was gradually weaned from all external feedback. Instead of being available continuously, the col-ored lights were inoperative every other minute, then three minutes out of every four, then seven minutes out of every eight. After that the patient was on his own. Presumably, he had learned to sense his PVCs through internal cues, and to bring his heart back to its normal pumping rhythm whenever something went wrong.

According to Engel and Weiss, five of the eight patients did learn to control their PVCs to some extent during the study. The most successful trainee was a middle-aged woman with very frequent PVCs and a long history of heart disease. During training, her PVCs virtually disappeared. Follow-up examinations indicated that irregular beats were still quite rare three years later; the drugs she had formerly taken to control her arrhythmia were no longer necessary, and she had had no further heart trouble.

The researchers asked the five successful patients to describe exactly what they did to stabilize their heart rates. Some said that they could stop their PVCs by slowing down the heart; others said that speeding it up was more effective. To make the heart beat slower, one patient said that she thought about swinging back and forth on a swing; another simply lay still and stared at the red light. To make the heart beat faster, one patient thought about "bouncing a rubber ball"; another imagined that she was arguing with her children or running down a dark street. The middle-aged woman mentioned above said that as soon as she sensed a PVC she "thought about relaxing," which somehow *speeded* up her heart and stabilized it.

The lack of consistency in these answers came as no surprise to Engel. Like Miller and other biofeedback researchers, he believes that what a person says he is doing to control his glands and internal organs may have no relation to what his nervous system is actually doing. From all the physiological evidence, Engel suspects that his trainees learned to stabilize their heart rhythm by directly modifying the firing rate of the vagus nerve. Whether or not their conscious use of mental imagery helped the heart patients achieve more precise control is anybody's guess. One patient showed a more stable heart rate after training, even though he had never learned to tell when a PVC was occurring. On the other hand, two of Engel's subjects learned to correct serious arrhythmias only after they came to realize what a normal heartbeat felt like. These patients were so accustomed to the sensations produced by a malfunctioning heart that they were actually frightened by a sequence of regular beats, which they took as a sign that something was wrong. Once their misconceptions were cleared up, both made rapid progress.

Heart disease and high blood pressure together account for one out of every five deaths in the United States each year. More than twenty-five million Americans—a fifth of the adult population—suffer from primary hypertension. Since this condition seems to be at least partly psychosomatic in origin, it is not surprising that a number of scientists in addition to Neal Miller have been searching for a way to teach hypertensives to lower their own pressure. The most promising results to date have come from a team of physiologists, psychologists, and physicians at the Harvard Medical School. In a recent clinical study conducted by Herbert Benson, David Shapiro, Bernard Tursky, and Gary E. Schwartz, seven hypertensive patients were trained to bring down their systolic pressure. Although all but one were taking anti-hypertensive drugs, their average systolic reading at the beginning of the experiment was 165, some 40 to 50 millimeters higher than normal.

Working independently of Miller and his associates, the Harvard team has devised a slightly different system of recording and rewarding changes in blood pressure. Instead of monitoring pressure on a heartbeat-by-heartbeat basis, this system uses an inflatable cuff to track the median pressure (either systolic or diastolic) over fifty consecutive beats. Each group of fifty beats is treated as one "trial." Cuff pressure is kept constant during each trial. Whenever the patient's systolic pressure falls below the cuff pressure, a light-and-tone signal is turned on for a split second. Although the patient does not know exactly what this signal represents, he has been told that it is something good and that he should try to make it appear. If the patient does this consistently during one trial, the cuff pressure is lowered for the next fifty heartbeats; this means that the patient has to lower his pressure still further to turn on the signal. As a bonus, after every twenty presentations of the light-and-tone signal, a photographic slide is flashed on a screen, informing the patient that he has just earned five cents.

To rule out placebo effects due to exposure to the experimental situation itself, the patients were first asked to sit through as many as sixteen "control sessions," in which blood pressure was recorded but no feedback or reinforcement was given. No changes in blood pressure were observed during this pre-training period.

The actual training sessions consisted of thirty trials each. Training was continued on a daily basis until no further reductions in systolic blood pressure occurred for five consecutive sessions. In these conditions, six of the seven patients showed decreases in systolic pressure ranging from 3.5 to 34 millimeters. One woman, who completed 33 sessions, dropped from 213.3 to 179.5. Although this is still far from normal, any substantial decrease in blood pressure reduces the strain on the cardiovascular system and presumably increases life expectancy. The Harvard researchers have also reported significant but smaller reductions in diastolic pressure during experiments with healthy (normotensive) subjects. The medical applications of this work are obvious—*if* the effects of the training can be sustained. So far the evidence is inconclusive, since Benson, Shapiro, Tursky, and Schwartz did not measure the blood pressure of the hypertensive patients outside the laboratory on any consistent basis, either during or after the training period.

"Sick headaches" are probably the most common of all psychosomatic complaints. Doctors recognize two basic kinds: migraines and tension headaches. The causes of migraine attacks are not fully understood, but the pain seems to be associated with excessive blood flow in the scalp region (*not* in the brain tissue itself); the pain of tension headaches comes from a chronic contraction of the skeletal muscles in the forehead and neck. Although such headaches do not kill anyone, the suffering they cause and the work days lost as a consequence make them a major health problem by any standard. Recently two separate teams of researchers have shown that biofeedback training can help people moderate or even suppress severe headache pain.

Improbable as it may sound, migraine sufferers have learned to turn off the pain in their head by warming up their hands "from the inside." This strange treatment was discovered more or less by accident at the Menninger Foundation in Topeka, Kansas, a few years ago. A group of Menninger scientists—psychologists Elmer E. Green and E. Dale Waters and internist Joseph D. Sargent—had been engaged in a far-ranging research program into unconventional methods of bodily control. One of their prize subjects was a forty-year-old Indian yogi named Swami Rama. The Swami, who had been practicing yoga since the age of four, had come to the United States at the urging of his guru, who felt that the time was ripe to demonstrate to Western medical scientists the benefits of a thoroughly disciplined nervous system. Green offered him a chance to show what he could do with a battery of instruments continuously monitoring his vital functions. The Swami was supremely confident of his abilities—and with good reason. The instruments showed that, without moving any of his skeletal muscles or changing his breathing, he could make his heart beat five times faster than normal—a pace that would be fatal if sustained. The Swami could also produce a 10-degree difference in skin temperature between the thumb and the little finger of his right hand. Green and his colleagues took a special interest in this latter performance. Skin temperature is primarily a function of local blood flow. A "hot flush" in a particular area indicates thoroughly dilated blood vessels; cold, clammy skin is a sign of tightly constricted blood vessels. During the Swami's demonstration one side of his palm became visibly flushed; the other side turned gray. He had apparently developed the ability to alter the flow of blood at will by dilating and contracting the two arteries that run through the wrist. When asked how he did this, the Swami explained that the first step in his long process of self-education was to concentrate on what he called "even breathing." He had practiced breathing slower and slower and slower until he was able to take as few as one or two breaths per minute for long periods of time without feeling discomfort. This rate of respiration is below the threshold where an involuntary reflex usually cuts in, forcing air into the lungs no matter how hard a person tries to hold his breath. But Swami Rama had trained himself to approach this threshold very gradually; and by taking care to inhale and exhale as smoothly as possible, he could in effect cross the border that separates voluntary from involuntary functions without triggering the respiratory reflex. Once he had made this breakthrough, he found it possible to gain control over heart rate, blood flow, and other vital functions usually regulated by reflex mechanisms.

Even before the Swami's visit, the Menninger scientists had been looking for a way to teach people with circulatory ailments to control the flow of blood through their arteries. The Swami proved that it could be done, but his training methods—which included years of meditation in a cave—were hardly applicable to Western medical practice. Green and his colleagues decided to see if they could achieve comparable results by combining biofeedback instrumentation with a self-hypnotic technique known as autogenic training. This form of mental and physical therapy was developed in the early 1900s by a German psychiatrist named Johannes Schultz, who was interested in both hypnosis and yoga. The basis of autogenic training—which is

widely used in European clinics—is a series of verbal for-
mulas that the subject repeats to himself to induce a state
of deep relaxation. Among the phrases recommended by
Schultz and his followers are: "I feel quite quiet . . . I am
beginning to feel quite relaxed . . . my feet feel heavy and
relaxed, my solar plexus and the whole central portion of
my body feel relaxed and quiet . . . my arms and hands are
heavy and warm . . . my hands are warm . . . warmth is
flowing into my hands, they are warm, warm . . ."

In adapting this technique to their own purposes, the
Menninger scientists attached temperature-sensing devices
to the hands of volunteer subjects, so that while the subjects were practicing their hand-warming exercises, the
slightest increase in skin temperature would be immediately displayed on an easy-to-read meter. This would reward their initial effort and presumably spur them on to
greater success. Purely by chance, one of the first subjects
recruited for the pilot study in "autogenic feedback training" was a Kansas housewife who suffered from migraines.
During a training session at the lab, this woman had a
migraine attack. The researchers allowed her to sit quietly
in a dark room, but they did not unhook her from the
recording equipment, and a few minutes later Green was
astonished to see the temperature meter jump 10 degrees,
indicating a tremendous surge of blood into the hands. On
questioning the woman, he found that her headache had
vanished at just that moment.

Following up this lead, Green, Walters, and Sargent
launched an experiment in which seventy migraine sufferers were given autogenic feedback training. More than two-
thirds of these subjects ended up with warmer hands and
fewer headaches. No one has explained exactly why the
treatment works, but there is some evidence that the blood
vessels in the head and the hands are on opposite sides of
a cardiovascular seesaw. When the vessels in the hands

contract, the vessels in the head dilate (as in a migraine attack), and when the balance is restored, the headache goes away. Normal hand temperature is around 90 degrees. On the first day of training, the migraine patients often arrived at the laboratory with hand temperatures around 70 degrees. Many of them learned to raise this temperature 15 or 20 degrees in a single session. They were then given portable temperature meters and told to continue practicing their autogenic exercises at home. Those subjects who managed to keep their hand temperatures close to normal —as measured in weekly check-ups at the lab—had fewer headaches, and when headaches did occur, they were able to moderate them. (Simply putting on gloves or holding one's hands over a fire will not help; the warming must come from the inside with a change in blood flow.)

Some of the successful subjects reported that their headache control was becoming more and more automatic as time went by. Green cites the case history of one woman, a computer programer, whose migraines were invariably preceded by what doctors call an aura. Her particular aura was an olfactory hallucination; before each attack she became aware of a strong ammonia-like smell. Early in her training the woman discovered that if she went home as soon as she sensed the aura, lay down on her bed, and practiced her warmth-and-relaxation exercises for an hour, the headache would go away before it became very painful. After a few months of training, she found that it was enough if she just sat down in her private office and did her exercises for fifteen minutes. Now, whenever she senses the aura, she simply gives the mental command, "Go back down, blood!" Presumably, her brain and body do the rest, because the headache passes and she is able to go on working.

Just as there is no theoretical limit to the involuntary functions that can be brought under control through biofeedback training, the same techniques can be used to *increase* the individual's control over skeletal muscles that are normally thought of as completely voluntary. For example, most people can wrinkle and unwrinkle their brows at will by contracting and relaxing the frontalis muscle in the forehead. But this muscle can also tighten up gradually— so gradually in fact that the individual is not aware that anything is happening. Unfortunately, the result of this constant muscular tension is impossible to ignore—a painful headache that may last weeks and even months. Even when people with tension headaches are told the cause of their trouble, they cannot simply relax their frontalis muscles, any more than a person can simply "will" away a painful leg cramp. But two psychologists at the University of Colorado Medical Center, Johann Stoyva and Thomas Budzynski, have demonstrated that the frontalis can be coaxed into relaxing with feedback from an electromyograph (EMG) machine, which records the electrical activity in skeletal muscle tissue.

What Stoyva and Budzynski did in the lab was to convert the EMG signals from the frontalis into a continuous chatter of click sounds. These clicks increased in frequency as muscular tension increased—so that the subject could literally hear how tight his forehead was. The subject's job was to slow down the clicks by progressively relaxing his frontalis muscle. Of the six subjects who went through biofeedback training in the laboratory and who diligently practiced relaxation at home, four showed significant improvement; they learned to recognize the warning signs of muscle tension and to turn off most of their headaches. An objective measure of their success was the fact that they were able to get through an average day with much less pain-killing medication than they had previously required. A year and a half later three of the subjects reported that the frequency and severity of their headaches had remained at a relatively low level. Two control groups of six subjects each, who were systematically exposed to various aspects of the experimental situation but who did not receive actual EMG feedback training, showed no significant improvement.

Since some part of the brain is involved in the regulation of every bodily function, the ultimate in biofeedback would be reliable information on the constantly changing electrical activity within specific brain structures. If this information were available, it would no longer be necessary to monitor muscles, organs, and glands throughout the body; the instructor could simply reinforce the appearance of EEG patterns that are known to accompany desired patterns of behavior. The problem, as we have seen with alpha-wave training, is to find a close correlation between specific brain waves and specific behavior. Alpha waves are easy enough to monitor (with the right equipment), but predicting how behavior will change as a result of alpha-wave training is not so easy. Similarly, even if one knows that the hypothalamus plays a major role in regulating hunger, it may be extremely difficult to detect momentary fluctuations in the hunger drive—as Neal Miller and his co-workers found out. The most dramatic medical application of EEG feedback training so far was reported in 1972 by psychologist Maurice B. Sterman of the Veterans Administration Hospital in Sepulveda, California.

To begin with, Sterman and his associates identified a particular pattern of electrical activity in the sensorimotor cortex—the part of the brain that controls movements of the skeletal muscles. This pattern, which has been labeled the sensorimotor rhythm (SMR), seems to be associated with muscular quietude. Subjects produce SMR waves when they are awake but completely motionless. (The sensorimotor rhythm, which originates in a specific region of the brain, should not be confused with the alpha rhythm, which is recorded over a much wider area.) The SMR was first discovered in cats. Sterman found that hungry cats with implanted electrodes could easily be trained to increase their SMR production if they were given food only when that pattern appeared in their electroencephalographic records. Instead of pawing around their cages looking for food, these trained animals would sit like statues, inhibiting all skeletal muscle activity until they were fed. Other experiments revealed that the cats who had been trained to produce a lot of SMR also became unusually resistant to drug-induced convulsions. This gave Sterman the idea of training epileptics, whose repeated seizures are thought to result from a breakdown of those components in the nervous system that normally inhibit muscular activity.

Preliminary tests on three epileptic patients have been highly encouraging. Standard feedback devices—lights, bells, pictures projected on a screen—were used to let the patients know when they were producing the right kind of brain wave. Once the patients had learned to increase their SMR production in the laboratory, their epileptic seizures became less frequent. In one case, that of a six-year-old boy, the results of the training were astonishing. The boy had been suffering as many as twenty-five seizures a week despite massive medication. When brought to the laboratory by his parents, he was so drugged and disordered that Sterman doubted his ability to comprehend even the simplest instructions. Yet after half a year of training the young patient had remained free of seizures for four months, and he was able to lead a relatively normal life on a much lower dosage of anticonvulsive drugs.

Perhaps because biofeedback research lends itself so easily to commercial exploitation, scientists in the field go to great lengths to avoid premature claims of success. Many of the pilot studies have been published in *Psychosomatic Medicine,* a journal whose editor, Dr. Morton F. Reiser, urges extreme caution in interpreting the results. With the exception of the tension-headache study, the research so far lacks the necessary controls to rule out placebo effects and other artifacts. Yet Reiser adds, "This is the way science always progresses, one small step at a time."

Ironically, much of the promising clinical work was stimulated by reports of Miller's success in training curarized rats to control their visceral functions—a success that Miller and his associates have since found difficult to repeat. For some reason, the experiments with curarized rats in the last few years have yielded steadily diminishing evidence of visceral learning, until the rats seem to have stopped learning entirely. At a meeting of the Eastern Psychological Association held in Boston in April 1972, Miller described the efforts that he and Dworkin were making to pinpoint the factor (or factors) behind what Miller calls "the extraordinarily perplexing dilemma of a persistent failure to replicate what previously seemed to be a robust phenomenon." One possibility they have looked into is a change in the chemical properties of the drug *d*-tubocurarine. After being told that the process of manufacturing this drug had not changed over the last few years, Miller and Dworkin learned that *d*-tubocurarine is actually an imperfectly purified natural product, and that different batches may vary in make-up, depending on the source of the material in the South American jungle—"much as wine varies with different vineyards and vintages." This raised the question of whether some impurity that was no longer present had somehow contributed to the original results. Miller is also exploring the possibility that significant changes may have been introduced into the strain of white rats his laboratory has been using. The companies that supply white rats for scientific research are constantly trying to improve their product. In recent years they have taken to breeding and raising their animals in absolutely sterile surroundings; they even get their foundation stock through Caesarean operation to guard against contamination by unwanted bacteria. According to Miller, it may be that these virtually stress-free conditions are preventing infant rats from developing their innate capacity for visceral learning. (There is independent evidence of physiological changes in the white-rat population since the visceral-learning experiments began; another scientist told Miller that the dose of male hormones needed to sterilize a newborn female rat is now almost ten times larger than that required a dozen years ago.) Closer to home, Miller and Dworkin discovered that the respiratory apparatus used in most of the earlier experiments was much less reliable than anyone thought; and they have had a new respirator built to their specifications.

Out of frustration, Miller says that he has even considered the possibility that he and the six researchers who collaborated with him on the early animal work were victims of a "mass hallucination." But he quickly adds that this hypothesis must take into account the fact that some of the key experiments were carried out under the supervision of other senior scientists, as well as the fact that at least two other laboratories in the late 1960s had no trouble replicating the visceral-learning effect. Miller, who has grappled with apparently insuperable research problems before, believes that he and his associates will eventually solve this one, and that the effort can only lead to a greater understanding of "the essential variables involved in visceral learning."

Meanwhile, the research with human subjects continues. In addition to trying to teach Robin Bielski to regain control over her diastolic pressure, Miller has initiated a unique experiment at Goldwater Memorial Hospital on Welfare Island in New York City. Here he and his colleagues are working with quadraplegic patients—victims of polio and other diseases that destroy the nerves controlling the skeletal muscles without affecting the neural control of the viscera. In theory, at least, the Goldwater patients have been left in a condition similar to that of the curarized rats in Miller's early animal experiments. And according to the same theory, these patients should learn to control their blood pressure more easily than ordinary subjects.

Besides serving as a test for Miller's basic research strategy, the Goldwater project may provide some practical pointers for increasing the efficiency of biofeedback training. As Miller sees it, there are several intriguing parallels between what curare does to rats and what experienced yogis do to themselves. "The yogis practice absolutely regular breathing, maintain a constant posture, and further rule out stimulus variability by monotonously concentrating their attention on a single point. The curarized rats have absolutely regular breathing, a constant posture, and a monotonous regularity of environmental cues because of both the paralysis and the sound-deadened box."

If his recent difficulties with the animal work can be resolved, and if it turns out that skeletal paralysis does indeed facilitate visceral learning, Miller envisions a less drastic method of duplicating curare's effect in the clinic. He suggests putting the subject in a "behavioral strait jacket." The subject would first be trained *not* to make respiratory and other skeletal responses that interfere with visceral learning. Only then would he be rewarded for the correct visceral response—which might be a reduction in blood pressure, a decrease in stomach contractions, or a change in heart rate. During the actual training, "any change in *skeletal* responses will automatically disconnect the reward circuit." In this way, distractions will be kept to a minimum and the subject will be forced to concentrate on the true therapeutic task—healing himself.

4

The Social Dimension

In a classic volume entitled *The Behavior of Organisms,* published in 1938, B. F. Skinner reached the conclusion that the autonomic nervous system could not be conditioned with trial-and-error learning techniques. In Skinner's view there were two distinct levels of complexity within the nervous system: on the more primitive level of the autonomic reflexes, only Pavlovian conditioning was effective; on the more sophisticated level of the somatic pathways, trial-and-error learning (or, as Skinner called it, "operant conditioning") came into play. In 1953 Skinner restated his opinion —which most of his colleagues had come to accept as orthodoxy—in even more emphatic language: "Glands and smooth muscles* do not naturally produce the kinds of consequences involved in operant conditioning, and when we arrange such consequences experimentally, operant conditioning does not take place. We may reinforce a man with food whenever he 'turns red' but we cannot in this way condition him to blush."

*The muscle tissue of visceral organs and blood vessels is called "smooth" in contrast to skeletal-muscle tissue, which shows regular striations or stripe-like markings under a microscope.

In 1968 Neal Miller and Leo P. DiCara published a report on their latest experiment with curarized rats. By rewarding dilation of blood vessels in specific parts of the body, Miller and DiCara not only had taught rats to "blush" on cue, they had taught some animals to blush in only one ear at a time. The successful demonstration of visceral learning in Miller's laboratory was a direct challenge to Skinner's concept of a split-level nervous system. In fact, Miller's work called into question Skinner's entire approach to the study of behavior. Although they are both behaviorists in the broad sense of the term, Miller and Skinner have had their share of disagreements in the professional journals. Skinner is far better known to laymen because of his knack for writing nontechnical books that vividly embody his ideas—*Walden Two* (1948) and *Beyond Freedom and Dignity* (1971). As a result, when behaviorists are portrayed in such popular works of art as *A Clockwork Orange,* or when intellectuals debate the influence of behaviorism on modern society, the image of the science presented is almost always pure Skinnerian. For most laymen, indeed, Skinner *is* behaviorism. But within the scientific community Miller is recognized as a formidable proponent of a markedly different approach to the study of behavior.

Ever since his apprenticeship under Clark Hull, Miller has been interested in the internal forces that motivate an organism to behave in a particular way at a particular time. As we have seen, his investigations of such drive states as hunger and fear led him deeper and deeper into the physiology of behavior and eventually into the neural circuitry of the brain itself. Taking advantage of the latest technical tools, he has tried to sort out what he calls the "central responses" that mediate all our actions, whether overt or internal, voluntary or involuntary.

By contrast, Skinner believes that the behaviorist should focus exclusively on overt, nonreflex actions. "We need a complete account [of such behavior] on the external level," he has written. "If I can't give a clear-cut formulation of a relationship between behavior and antecedent variables, it is no help to me to speculate about something inside the organism which will fill the gap." Skinner is no more interested in "drive states" than he is in "mental states." He considers both to be "psychological fictions" that divert the scientist from a truly objective study of behavior. What we should be looking at, he insists, is the *rate* at which a particular response is performed, and his goal, he says, is "to identify that rate as a function of manipulable, demonstrable conditions."

A newborn infant who has not been fed for three hours begins to cry; the mother rushes to feed it, and the baby quiets down. Another newborn baby begins to cry under similar circumstances, but the mother ignores it until the next scheduled feeding an hour later. If we consider only those factors that we can observe directly, we might predict that at the age of one month the first baby will be more likely to cry after three hours of food deprivation than the second baby. In Skinnerian terms, the two infants are operating under differently arranged "contingencies of reinforcement," and the job of the behaviorist, according to Skinner, is to analyze the effect of such contingencies on response rates. It might seem more appropriate to begin by saying that both babies cry "because they are hungry," and then try to define what we mean by that phrase. But Skinner argues that no one ever sees "hunger" as such; all we ever see is the crying and the eating and the quieting down—and all we really need to know is how these responses are functionally related to each other and to the environment. As Skinner puts it, "Behavior is shaped and maintained by its consequences." If the consequences can be observed and manipulated directly, why bother with hypothetical constructs like "hunger," which seem to offer explanations but which actually raise more questions than they answer?

Essentially Skinner is saying that it is not necessary to understand *why* a baby cries and eats; the goal of behaviorism is to be able to predict when he will cry and when he will eat. Miller would agree that all behaviorists must work toward accurate prediction, but, unlike Skinner, he sees no reason to tie one hand behind his back in pursuit of this enormously difficult goal.

Imagine for a moment an electronics engineer confronted with a mysterious "black box" that transforms certain inputs into certain outputs. The engineer's job is to figure out exactly what the device will do under any conceivable circumstance. Merely by observing it in action for a while, the engineer should be able to make one or two simple predictions: for example, every time a bell rings and one piece of the device is lifted into the air, strange voices can be heard. If the engineer is allowed to manipulate the gadget himself, he will probably be able to increase the range and accuracy of his predictions. For example, once he learns that the perforated dial on the front can be turned clockwise with one finger, he may go on to discover which combinations of turns produce women's voices, intermittent buzzing sounds, a continuous high-pitched hum, and so on. If the engineer had *unlimited* time and resources, he might continue experimenting until his predictions approached 100-per-cent accuracy. But he could probably save himself a lot of trouble by grabbing a screwdriver, prying open the bottom of the device, and taking a good look at the circuitry inside. There is no guarantee, of course, that such a breakthrough will clear up *all* the mysteries of the black box. The engineer may misinterpret what he sees and jump to false conclusions. Errors of this kind are especially likely if the black box turns out to be not a standard telephone but a complex servomechanism with multiple feedback loops and an elaborate set of programed instructions in an unfamiliar code. Nevertheless, the potential advantages far outweigh the potential disadvantages, since the engineer's chances of mastering a really complex black box *without* a glance at the circuitry are virtually nil.

Even Skinner's severest critics can admire the purity of his intellectual position. By refusing to deal with behavior on anything but the "external level," he has contributed greatly to our understanding of how past consequences shape future actions. But his intentionally limited perspective also led him to close the door on the possibility of visceral learning. And when Miller and others demonstrated that such learning was possible—and possibly beneficial—they struck a blow for a more eclectic, open-minded science of behavior.

The most surprising thing about this controversy over the "proper" research strategy is that it should ever have arisen in a field like behavioral psychology. From all appearances, the human nervous system is the most complicated black box in the universe, and we might expect the scientists confronting it to be grateful for *any* clues to its operating principles. The Russian scientists who followed in Pavlov's footsteps have certainly not hesitated to apply their knowledge of neural circuitry to behavioral research. Since this strategy appears to make such good sense, we are forced to ask why some of the most eminent American behaviorists have resisted it. One possible answer can be found in the writings of David Bakan, a professor of psychology at the University of Toronto, who offers a deadpan historical analysis of the behavior of John B. Watson, the founder of American behaviorism.

In an article entitled "Behaviorism and American Urbanization," Bakan takes off from Watson's own description of behavioral psychology as "purely an American production." He notes that in Watson's day (1919) this phrase commonly referred *not* to the country as a whole but to a particular section of it, rural and small-town America, where the traditional values were still preserved in contrast to the polyglot turmoil of the big cities. Watson himself was a product of rural South Carolina. Born in 1878, he was raised in a very religious family and slated for the ministry. Although he did poorly in local schools, he went on to Furman College and then to graduate school at the University of Chicago. Along the way, he took what Bakan describes as a "deep plunge into intellectuality," devouring everything he could read in philosophy and psychology.

Most historians have viewed Watson's decision to concentrate on the study of external behavior as a reaction against the sterile introspective methods of nineteenth-century psychology. But this decision can also be interpreted as a symptom of the general "depersonalization" that spread through American life in the wake of what Bakan calls "the urban encounter." Writing in 1924, Watson himself was quite explicit about the connection between behaviorism and the problems of city life:

> Civilized nations are rapidly becoming city dwellers. . . . If we are ever to learn to live together in the close relationships demanded by modern social and industrial life, we shall have to leave behind for a time our interest in chemistry and physics and even our interest in physiology and medicine, and enter upon a study of modern psychology.
>
> Fortunately, psychology is prepared to help us. The past ten years have seen the development of new points of view in psychology—points of view that have grown up partly to meet our ever-changing social needs and partly because the very existence of these needs has made a new viewpoint possible. . . . Behavioristic psychology . . . contends that the most fruitful starting point for psychology is the study not of our own self, but of our neighbor's behavior.

Bakan remarks that Watson's attitude is essentially that of "a country boy . . . looking on at the activities of people in the big city who are culturally alien to him." Actually, Watson did not spend much time studying human behavior at all. "I never wanted to use human subjects," he once admitted. "I hated to serve as a subject. . . . I was always uncomfortable and acted unnaturally. With animals I was at home." A fellow graduate student at the University of Chicago remembers that Watson had "difficulty in making consistent introspective reports . . . some of us speculated in later years as to whether this fact may not have supplied some of the urge which eventually drove him toward a purely behavioristic system."

It is not necessary to adopt a psychoanalytical viewpoint to realize that Watson often tended to confuse his working hypotheses, his empirical data, and his personal predilections. Such confusion may be considered an unavoidable occupational hazard in a field where the investigator is also a member of the species under investigation. But whereas Freud and his followers at least recognized the danger and tried—however unsuccessfully—to overcome it, Watson and his followers insisted on the purely objective nature of their findings. To get a glimpse of the preconceptions that lay behind this "objectivity," we can turn to Watson's popular writings, where he was free to express himself without the restraints imposed by the professional journals.

At the beginning of his famous handbook for parents, *Psychological Care of Infant and Child* (1928), Watson strikes what sounds like a sober, modest note: "No one today knows enough to raise a child." But it soon becomes clear that Watson means "no one without the *proper scientific training,*" because he goes on to claim that a human infant can be easily molded by adults who have the knowledge and the power to control the child's environment. "We are forced to believe from the study of facts," says the university-professor-turned-advertising-executive, "that . . . there are no instincts. We build in at an early age everything that is later to appear." The "facts" that Watson found so impressive in reaching this conclusion came from a handful of experiments with newborn infants. The purpose of these studies was to see whether certain reactions commonly regarded as "instinctive"—such as fear of fire and fear of furry animals—could be elicited from completely naïve subjects. The results convinced Watson that there are only two innate fears: fear of loud noises and fear of falling. All other fears must be regarded as "homemade." To back up this assertion, Watson offers the lay reader a brief description of a typical experiment: A live rabbit is placed on a blanket next to a nine-month-old infant. The child reaches out immediately to pet the animal. "But just as his hands touch it," Watson writes, "I bang a steel bar [with a hammer] behind his head. He whimpers and cries and shows fear." After the child has quieted down, the rabbit is placed on the blanket again. This time the child reacts "quite slowly. . . . Finally he does touch it gingerly." Again the steel bar is struck with the hammer. Again the child recoils. When the rabbit is presented a third time, "something new develops. No longer do I have to rap the steel bar behind his head to bring out fear. He shows fear at the sight of the rabbit. . . . He begins to cry and turn away the moment he sees it."

To explain how such Pavlovian goings-on can affect our lives outside the laboratory, Watson conjures up a scenario of a child alone in a dark room night after night, being conditioned to fear the darkness by a cacophony of slamming doors, falling screens, dropped pots and pans, and cracks of thunder. "All of these things are powerful agents," Watson warns, "they are sledgehammers in the shaping of your child."

If this scenario is somewhat less convincing than the experiment on which it is based, it is positively persuasive compared to Watson's scientific analysis of the shaping of the infant's love life. He begins with the simple statement: "Our laboratory studies show that we can bring out a love response in a newborn child by just one stimulus—*by stroking its skin.*" He then proceeds to show how this innate "love response" can become attached, through an ever-lengthening chain of conditioning, to the mother's face (which the child sees when he is being stroked), to the sound of the mother's voice, to the sound of her footsteps, to the sight of her clothes, and even to her photograph on the dresser. At this point Watson can hardly contain his disgust at the way things are going. "All too soon," he says, "the child gets shot through with too many of these love reactions. In addition the child gets honeycombed with love responses for the nurse, for the father, and for any other constant attendant who fondles it. Love reactions soon dominate the child." This is presumably a bad thing. But the reader will look in vain for any documentation of Watson's next statement—that the end result of "overcoddling" in childhood is the dreadful condition in adults that he calls "invalidism" and that he defines as a morbid concern with "every little ill," especially "our elimination processes, and the like." He goes on to complain, "You can see invalidism in the making in the majority of American homes," where children learn that they can get all the petting and kissing they crave by reporting every physical ailment, no matter how minor, to their doting mother. Fortunately, Watson has a scientific solution to this problem. He offers it to parents under the heading: "Should the mother never kiss the baby?"

> There is a sensible way of treating children. Treat them as though they were young adults. Dress them, bathe them with

care and circumspection. Let your behavior always be objective and kindly firm. Never hug and kiss them, never let them sit in your lap. If you must, kiss them once on the forehead when they say good night. Shake hands with them in the morning. Give them a pat on the head if they have made an extraordinarily good job of a difficult task. Try it out. In a week's time you will find how easy it is to be perfectly objective with your child and at the same time kindly. You will be utterly ashamed of the mawkish, sentimental way you have been handling it.

The mind reels at the thought of what Dr. Spock would say to parents who instituted such a regime today. This is not to imply that modern child psychologists have all the answers. Given the current state of knowledge in this field, most theories about child-rearing must be considered no better than half-educated guesses. But *some* progress has been made since the 1920s, and it is quite clear that Watson's dogmatic pronouncements have not stood the test of time. Experiments with monkey infants have confirmed what most parents knew all along: that lots of body contact and stroking is essential to the normal physical and social development of young primates. Without constant "mothering," the little monkeys grow up sickly, insecure, and either overly timorous or irrationally aggressive. Similar defects have been observed in adequately nourished but otherwise neglected children in understaffed foundling homes. Furthermore, the work of modern ethologists such as Konrad Lorenz has brought a new respectability to what used to be called "instinct theory." Studying animals in their natural habitat rather than in a laboratory, Lorenz and others have shown how unlearned patterns of behavior— complex responses common to all members of a species— can be triggered or "released" in an individual by certain stimuli. For example, it is the cheeping of her chicks that releases maternal behavior in the mother hen. A brooding turkey hen will mother any object, including a stuffed fox or weasel, that "cheeps" like a turkey chick. Yet once the same hen is deafened by surgery, she will peck her own chicks to death if they approach the empty nest she is "defending." The application of ethological findings to human behavior remains controversial. But such developmental psychologists as Jean Piaget and Jerome Kagan have also stressed the importance of innate abilities that gradually come into play as brain and body mature; they argue that biological developments not only determine what the individual is able to learn at each stage of growth but also how he perceives the world around him. To put it bluntly, the child is *not* a little adult, and it would be disastrous to treat him as such.

Watson can hardly be blamed for not anticipating the discoveries of his successors. But the almost heroic wrongness of some of his guesses—coupled with his failure even to frame certain questions—points to a more basic flaw in his approach to the scientific study of behavior. This is best illustrated in another example taken from *Psychological Care of Infant and Child.* Along with most medical authorities of his day, Watson believed that thumb-sucking was "unsocial," "auto-erotic," and possibly injurious to health. He assumed that the habit began as a "conditioned response connected with eating," and that therefore the best time to "cure" it was "during the first few days of infancy." His suggested remedy: "Keep the hands away from the mouth as often as you are near the baby during its waking moments. And always when you put it into its crib for sleep, see that the hands are tucked inside the covers." If habitual thumb-sucking develops "in spite of this early scrutiny," more drastic measures are called for: "Sew loose white canton flannel mitts with no finger or thumb divisions to the sleeves of the night gown and on all the *day dresses, and leave them on for two weeks or more—day and night.* So many mothers leave them on only at night. Unless the child is watched every moment, the hand will at one time or another get back to the mouth. . . . If the habit still persists, make the mitts of rougher and rougher material" (Watson's italics).

Even if we reserve judgment on whether thumb-sucking is "bad" for the child, we cannot help being put off by the arrogance with which Watson leaps from tentative prediction to omniscient control. Most upsetting, perhaps, is Watson's failure to ask himself: 1) Why does the infant try so hard to get his hand to his mouth? 2) Can such a powerful habit be suppressed without causing problems in some other area of behavior? 3) Even if the fingerless mitts do the trick, is direct manipulation the *best* way to deal with this situation? Suppose that instead of adhering to a purely external definition of the problem, the behaviorist tries to form a hypothesis about the "drive" that thumb-sucking seems to satisfy in a child. One possibility to be considered is that every child is born with a physiological need for sucking—a trait that could have appeared in the course of evolution to ensure that the infant gets enough to eat at the breast. Or the behaviorist might think in terms of a general craving for oral stimulation acquired through the kind of conditioning process that Watson himself alludes to. Either way, once he assumes that thumb-sucking persists because it satisfies a strong drive, he can begin to weigh the relative merits of different methods of control. These may range from complete suppression of the offending behavior— slapping the child whenever he brings his thumb to his mouth and keeping him in a strait jacket when he can't be watched—to channeling his sucking response into a socially acceptable outlet through an array of positive reinforcements—teething rings, pacifiers, hard pretzels, et cetera. With the help of a sophisticated drive theory, we might even wish to consider a more radical alternative: doing nothing at all. Since the habit is motivated by a drive we can't control, we might decide to let the infant suck his thumb as long as he wants to, on the assumption that he will · stop of his own accord as soon as the drive diminishes.

Even in a relatively simple case like this one, it will not be easy to choose one course of action from the alternatives suggested by a thorough behavioral analysis. But that is exactly the point. Good scientific theories generate hard research problems. Any theory that oversimplifies in the name of objectivity will eventually interfere with scientific progress. And the mischief caused by an inadequate theory is especially insidious in the behavioral sciences, where ethical and practical considerations often rule out properly controlled experiments on human subjects. It is all too easy for the behaviorist to justify his preconceptions about human behavior with a few selected analogies from animal experiments. One great virtue of drive theory, as expounded by Clark Hull and rigorously developed by Neal Miller, is that it forces the behaviorist to go beyond these often misleading analogies and to look into the complexities of the "black box" itself. Once he starts trying to relate external behavior to what he sees inside the organism, oversimplification will no longer be his problem.

Watson himself said that a behaviorist should be well versed in physiology and neurology. But he was best known for such statements as: "The behaviorist recognizes no such things as mental traits, dispositions or tendencies." And there is no doubt that his influence helped to make the study of *external* behavior the primary concern of experimental psychology. Skinner's theoretical position is even clearer than Watson's. Skinner does not try to hide his impatience with physiology and neurology. Since he does not care what "causes" behavior, he rejects the Pavlovian stimulus-response framework that Watson found so useful. He is not interested in "reflexes," whether natural or conditioned. As he puts it, "The environment not only prods or lashes, it *selects*. Once this fact is recognized, we can formulate the interaction between organism and environment in a much more comprehensive way." The strict Skinnerian will argue that if Watson's prescription for controlling thumb-sucking does not work, this simply proves that Watson's analysis of the reinforcement contingencies was inadequate. Since all behavior, no matter how complex, "is shaped and maintained by its consequences," there is no need to look under the skin of the organism for additional information. Of course, there are many examples of complex behavior—in rats and pigeons as well as in human beings—that we cannot yet predict and control as precisely as we would like. But the Skinnerian assumes that these cases will eventually yield to a "scientific analysis of behavior"—if not tomorrow, then the day after.

This assumption—which is not so much a working hypothesis as an article of faith—may indeed turn out to be correct. But Skinner's attempt to show the way in his most recent book for laymen, *Beyond Freedom and Dignity,* does not inspire much confidence. His basic argument is that the time has come to apply the insights of behavioral psychology to large-scale social engineering. To critics who maintain that these insights are still inadequate for the purpose, Skinner asks: What alternative is there? The old order is breaking down, and we have no choice but to turn to "a technology of operant behavior" which, he says, is "already well advanced and may prove to be commensurate with our problems." To critics who fear that behavioral technology may be *too* successful—that it may lead to a new kind of totalitarianism—Skinner asks: How can the scientific control of behavior produce a worse world than the one we have now? After all, behavioral technology is a tool like any other: Dictators may use it to oppress the masses; democracies may use it to promote the greatest good for the greatest number.

Over and over, Skinner repeats one point: *All* freedom is an illusion, our minds and bodies are already "controlled," partly through biology and partly through contingencies of reinforcement that have been arranged by forces outside us. These forces include elements of the natural environment—climate, geography, and so forth—as well as the actions of other people, who are themselves controlled by the same behavioral mechanisms. The only difference between the slave and the free man is that the latter dances on less conspicuous strings. Once we accept the idea that all freedom is an illusion, Skinner says, we can formulate a scientifically sound policy for good government. The goal is not to "break our chains"—a meaningless slogan—but to use behavioral technology to rearrange the contingencies of reinforcement so that all men will *necessarily* become happier and healthier: "What is needed is more intentional control, not less, and this is an important engineering problem."

Skinner calls his book *Beyond Freedom and Dignity* because he wants to impress on the reader that these two words have no meaning in the context of modern behavioral science. They are relics of a prescientific era, when it was still possible to believe in "autonomous man"—an individual who was ultimately responsible for all his actions because he came equipped with a "free will" that remained untouched by biological and environmental factors. The last hundred years have seen a steady erosion of this concept. Marx, Darwin, Freud—each in his way made it harder for us to believe in autonomous man. Now Skinner asks: If we can accept the idea that we are not truly autonomous, which kind of control is preferable—to be manipulated by "blind nature," or by a social engineer who is carrying out a carefully designed plan for human betterment?

Even the most ardent defenders of freedom and dignity reserve the right to "change men's minds" by rational dis-

course; and Skinner goes on to equate this kind of persua-
sion with the methods of behavioral control he recom-
mends. For example, we might urge on a dawdler by saying, "Look what time it is!" What we are really doing,
according to Skinner, is trying to increase the probability
that a certain kind of behavior will occur by pointing to the
possibly aversive consequences of *not* behaving that way.
We also try to change a person's behavior by pointing to
the possibly rewarding consequences of a certain course of
action, as in the phrases "Act like a man" or "Honesty is
the best policy." Since *all* behavior is controlled in one way
or another, the real argument between humanism and
behaviorism is over different kinds of control—weak or
strong, inconspicuous or conspicuous, culturally approved
or culturally condemned. Changing someone else's mind is
condoned by the defenders of freedom and dignity because
it is an "ineffective way of changing behavior," while
" 'brainwashing' is proscribed . . . simply because the control is obvious."

To make his point even clearer, Skinner says that "urging
and persuading are effective only if there is already some
tendency to behave." And he tries to reassure the humanist
by explaining that when a social engineer rearranges the
contingencies of reinforcement, he is bound to rely mostly
on positive reinforcements—rewards rather than punishments—because rewards are much more effective in controlling behavior. For the humanist, however, the difference between persuading and brainwashing is precisely
that the persuader does *not* rearrange the contingencies of
reinforcement; he simply takes advantage of what is there.
In other words, he draws his power to change behavior
from the culture and the environment; he does not wield
it directly. This is a subtle but crucial distinction. What
Skinner fails to see is that the widespread resistance to
social engineering is based not on a primitive fear of behav-

ioral manipulation *per se,* but on a perfectly rational fear of the corrupting influence of power. Once the social engineers are given the power to rearrange contingencies of reinforcement in our name, what will prevent them from turning such power to their own purposes?

Unfortunately, just at the point where we need the most sophisticated behavioral analysis, Skinner lets us down. And his failure—which is fatal to a polemical work of this kind—can be traced directly to his refusal to consider what happens *inside* the behaving organism. Skinner keeps protesting that his Utopian vision is not totalitarian because the new society will be a product of exactly the same forces that have shaped every society since the beginning of civilization. He concedes that new reinforcement contingencies will have to be designed by specialists, and that there may be an awkward transition period, but he sees no reason why a democratic society cannot take steps to ensure that the social engineers always remain under the control of the reinforcement mechanisms they themselves design. Stimulus-response learning theory, however, suggests at least one good reason for pessimism.

To protect itself against antisocial acts, a democratic society must rely on agreed-upon ethical codes, which are inculcated in the young as soon as possible and then continually reinforced by such official and quasi-official institutions as churches, schools, political parties, and the press. If these reinforcers lose their effectiveness, habits based on early learning encounters may begin to fade—and other kinds of responses will come to the surface. Learning theory leads us to expect that in any transitional period innate motivational factors—that is, primary drives—will become more important in determining what a person does from moment to moment. And history confirms that this is exactly what happens to conquering soldiers and triumphant revolutionaries. Once the normal behavioral restraints are removed, or greatly weakened by social upheavals, perfectly ordinary citizens become capable of extraordinary antisocial acts—rape, looting, murder—just as if they had never been exposed to the usual civilizing influences in childhood. The social engineer may not be freed from the restraints of civilization quite so dramatically as the conquering soldier or the triumphant revolutionary. But, like them, he will be set above the everyday reinforcing mechanisms—at least temporarily. And the more tinkering he does with the basic system of rewards and punishments in his society, the closer he approaches to the role of Omnipotent Outsider—and the more difficult it will be to predict his behavior in terms of the normal social parameters.

While we rightly tremble at the prospect of a Skinnerian technocracy, we can at least be grateful to Skinner for defining the problem in such vivid terms. Having brought the world to the brink of destruction, we cannot afford to leave the future to blind nature or mere accident. And those who believe that society needs redesigning must make use of whatever tools behavioral psychology provides. But for this very reason we cannot be satisfied with Skinner's formulation. It is as much a matter of emphasis as anything else. What we need is a science of behavior that will tell us not just how to control others, but how to control ourselves. If we are lucky, we may get it in time.

Index

Index